the pink
COOKBOOK

the pink
COOKBOOK

over 200 feel-good recipes

hamlyn

An Hachette Livre UK Company

First published in Great Britain in 2007 by
Hamlyn, a division of Octopus Publishing Group Ltd
2-4 Heron Quays, London E14 4JP

ISBN-13: 978-0-600-61715-0
ISBN-10: 0-600-61715-7

A CIP catalogue record for this book is available from the British Library

Printed and bound in Dubai

10 9 8 7 6 5 4 3 2 1

Note

Both metric and imperial measurements are given for the
recipes. Use one set of measures only, not a mixture of both.

This book includes dishes made with nuts and nut derivatives. It
is advisable for those with known allergic reactions to nuts and
nut derivatives and those who may be potentially vulnerable to
these allergies, such as pregnant and nursing mothers, invalids,
the elderly, babies and children, to avoid dishes made with nuts
and nut oils. It is also prudent to check the labels of preprepared
ingredients for the possible inclusion of nut derivatives.

Meat and poultry should be cooked thoroughly. To test if poultry
is cooked, pierce the flesh through the thickest part with a
skewer or fork – the juices should run clear, never pink or red.

A note from Breast Cancer Care

This is a collection of uplifting recipes from well-known chefs,
celebrities and people who have been affected by breast
cancer. They have personally chosen the recipes because they
are important to them as individuals and have donated them to
support Breast Cancer Care through fundraising. This
cookbook is not intended as a guide for healthy eating,
reducing the risk of cancer or a route to weight loss and any
desserts or recipes containing high fat or sugar products should
be considered as treats to be consumed in moderation.

The recipes are not to be confused with foods that would
reduce the chances of developing breast cancer. There is, as
yet, no scientific evidence to suggest that food or diet can be
linked to an increased or decreased risk of breast cancer.

Overall, Breast Cancer Care encourages people to lead a
healthy lifestyle by taking regular exercise and enjoying a well
balanced, moderated diet.

Breast Cancer Care encourages women to be breast aware.
Men need to be breast aware too as nearly 350 men are
diagnosed every year in the UK. Being breast aware means
knowing how your breasts look and feel normally so that you
notice any changes quickly and report them to your doctor.
While most breast changes will be benign, early detection can
mean more effective treatment if the cancer is discovered during
initial stages.

The breast awareness 5-point code:
1 Know what is normal for you
2 Know what changes to look and feel for
3 Look and feel
4 Report any changes to your GP without delay
5 Attend routine breast screening if you are aged 50 and over

 the flower symbol represents a recipe that
has been contributed by someone whose
life has been touched by breast cancer and
some of their images appear on the inside
covers of this book

contents

foreword

As an Ambassador of the UK's leading breast cancer support charity, Breast Cancer Care, I was delighted to be invited to write the foreword for this book. It's not often that you see recipes from famous chefs and celebrities sitting next to well-loved dishes from everyday people. What makes it even more special is that these people have all been affected by breast cancer, and they are now offering up their favourite recipes in a bid to raise funds that can be used to support others.

By buying this book you are contributing to Breast Cancer Care's invaluable work and supporting the thousands of people who are affected by breast cancer every day.

This cookbook is also a wonderful opportunity to treat those you love to over 200 delicious recipes and a perfect excuse to get families and friends together for a meal.

When I was diagnosed with breast cancer in 2001 I realized just how important it was to have family and friends around me for comfort and support. My diagnosis left me feeling shocked, empty and uncertain. It was difficult not knowing what to expect and how I would be affected. For example, I was amazed to discover that four hours after my first chemotherapy session my taste buds had dramatically changed. I started yearning for light, fresh, pure tastes, with texture becoming all-important. Although I had lost my appetite, just

planning meals helped me get through the four long months of treatment. It gave me something to look forward to and gave my day some stability. The recipe for *Sea Bass Baked in Salt* (see pages 58-59) that I have donated for this book became a real favourite for me during this time because it is a simple dish with a delicious taste and texture.

My experience of breast cancer also made me realize how important it is for people diagnosed and their families to have access to the type of practical information and emotional support that Breast Cancer Care offers. There were several unexpected side-effects that I just wasn't prepared for. Although my taste has now returned, I was very concerned at the time as it's my livelihood, and I didn't know whether it would be a permanent effect of treatment. Fortunately, Breast Cancer Care is there to answer all these types of questions and to help people every step of the way, from the moment they are diagnosed, throughout their treatment and as they build a life after breast cancer.

I became the charity's Ambassador in 2003 because I truly admire and value the work that they do, helping thousands of people and their friends and families deal with life after a breast cancer diagnosis. During treatment I experienced hair loss, which doesn't do

much for a woman's self-confidence. When I learned of Breast Cancer Care's Headstrong service, which offers help on how to cope with hair loss as well as teaching different scarf-tying and headwear techniques, I thought what a fantastic way it was to help people regain their self-esteem. In a range of different ways, Breast Cancer Care makes a really meaningful difference to the lives of people affected by breast cancer.

Thank you again to all of the keen cooks who have contributed to *The Pink Cookbook: Over 200 Feel-good Recipes*. Your support will help Breast Cancer Care to continue to provide free and confidential information and support to people affected by breast cancer anywhere in the UK.

Enjoy this cookbook and all the wonderful dinner parties and friendships that will follow!

Rose Gray, Co-founder of the River Café

introduction

' The most important thing is to enjoy your life – to be happy – that's all that matters. '
Audrey Hepburn

Congratulations! You've just bought this book, and, by so doing, you are directly giving £1 to help Breast Cancer Care continue its invaluable work.

Breast cancer is the most common cancer in the UK, with nearly 44,000 women and 350 men newly diagnosed each year. Without the support of people like you, Breast Cancer Care wouldn't be able to help the growing number of people affected by breast cancer, and some people would have to face their journey through diagnosis and treatment alone and unsupported. The money raised for the charity helps to fund the training and delivery of all its emotional and practical support services that are offered free to anybody who needs them.

Within these pages you'll find recipes for every occasion, from the *BLT Sandwich* (see page 27), perfect the day after a big night out, to a *Strawberry and Pineapple Smoothie* (see page 13), which is packed with vitamins and minerals to enjoy before you head off for a session at the gym. On days that

challenge you, try a comforting bowl of *Indian Lamb with Almond Sauce* (see page 54) or tangy *Chicken with Lemon Grass and Asparagus* (see page 46). The Light Bites and Quick and Easy chapters contain plenty of appetizing dishes, including classic E*ggs Florentine* (see page 94) and creamy *Pumpkin Soup with Harissa* (see page 84), which are great when you're busy but still want to eat well.

Vegetarians and meat-eaters alike will adore the delicious and nutritious ideas in Simply Veggie, while the recipes in the Girls' Night In chapter provide the perfect excuse to get the girls round! Kick off those high heels, pour yourself a *Pink Melon Delight* (see page 153) or a *Cosmopolitan* (see page 154) and tuck into a tasty *Mediterranean Pasta Bake* (see page 135) or a *Salmon Tart with Wholegrain Mustard and Rocket* (see page 136). Finish off with a slice of *Rich Chocolate Cake* (see page 148) or a refreshing *Papaya and Lime Salad* (see page 152).

Take our quick World Tour and you will find everything from *Sushi* (see page 170) to *Thai Chicken Salad* (see page 161), classic *Moussaka* (see page 172) and simply irresistible *White Chocolate Biscotti* (see page 178). One of the ways to a man's heart is said to be through cooking, and the quick and easy recipes in A Little Romance mean more time with your loved-one. Home-cooked *Fillet Steak with Mustard Sauce* (see page 186) and *Lemon and Passion Fruit Tart with Raspberries* (see page 199) are an ideal combination. And why not make life even sweeter for you and yours with *Green Tea Ice Cream* (see pages 206-207) or a traditional *Lemon Drizzle Cake* (see page 214)? Finally, celebrate with a *Classic Pimm's* cocktail (see page 248) or *Kiwifruit, Grape and Lime Crush* (see page 248) accompanied by stylish *Cherry Tomato Tartlets* (see page 244).

Savour and enjoy the recipes in this book and keep yourself in good shape to live life to the full by taking plenty of exercise and maintaining a well-balanced diet with a few treats and healthy snacks along the way. Drink plenty of water and watch your alcohol consumption but have fun and, as Breast Cancer Care will tell you, be breast aware and follow the 5-point code (see page 4). As the ultimate diva Mae West once said: 'You only live once, but if you do it right, once is enough'.

early bird

From quick-fix juices and smoothies to ideas for leisurely weekend brunches, this selection of recipes will make getting up in the morning a more pleasurable experience. Try a *Raw Energy* juice for a speedy breakfast that's packed full of vitamins or take your time with the Indian inspired *Kipper Kedgeree*.

*D*iana Moran's
green goddess healthy juice

PREP: 10 MINUTES
NO COOK
MAKES: 200 ML (7 FL OZ)
SERVES: 1

175 g (6 oz) melon (about ¼ large melon) peeled

125 g (4 oz) cucumber

125 g (4 oz) avocado, peeled and stoned

50 g (2 oz) dried apricots, plus extra to decorate (optional)

1 tablespoon wheatgerm

2 ice cubes

Juice the melon and cucumber. If you do this in a blender, sieve to extract the juice, taking care not to push the purée through.

Put the melon and cucumber into a blender with the avocado, apricots, wheatgerm and a couple of ice cubes and whiz together. Serve decorated with dried apricot slivers, if liked.

' I support *The Pink Cookbook* because I have had breast cancer myself and want to help and encourage other women and their families facing the disease, and show them that there is life after cancer. '

strawberry and pineapple
smoothie

PREP: 5 MINUTES, PLUS FREEZING
NO COOK
MAKES: 2

150 g (5 oz) strawberries, hulled,
    plus extra slices to decorate
150 ml (¼ pint) pineapple juice
150 ml (¼ pint) strawberry yogurt
ice cubes, to serve

Get an energy boost and make one of these smoothies as a light breakfast before participating in one of **Breast Cancer Care's** Ribbon Walks. You can experience some of the most beautiful parts of the countryside by taking part in either a 10-mile or 20-mile walk. The walks, which usually take place in June, are designed to be great fun and challenging but achievable. To find out dates and locations for the next Ribbon Walk visit www.breastcancercare.org.uk.

Roughly chop the strawberries and put them in the freezer for at least 2 hours or overnight.

Blend the frozen strawberries, pineapple juice and yogurt until smooth.

Pour the mixture into 2 glasses, add a couple of ice cubes to each and top with more strawberries.

morning glory

PREP: 5 MINUTES
NO COOK
MAKES: 300 ML (½ PINT)

½ melon, preferably cantaloupe
ice cubes, to serve

Juice the melon flesh and seeds.

Serve over ice as an enlivening breakfast drink.

raw energy

PREP: 5 MINUTES
NO COOK
MAKES: 200 ML (7 FL OZ)

1 small tomato, about 100 g
    (3½ oz), plus extra to garnish
    (optional)
200 g (7 oz) cabbage
large handful of parsley
1 celery stick, to garnish (optional)

Juice the tomato, cabbage and parsley together.

Pour into a tumbler and serve garnished with sliced tomatoes or a stick of celery, if liked.

mango, coconut and
lime lassi

PREP: 10 MINUTES
NO COOK
MAKES: 2–4

1 large, ripe mango, deseeded,
    peeled and diced
juice of 1 orange
juice of 1 lime
1 tablespoon clear honey
300 ml (½ pint) plain yogurt
4 tablespoons coconut milk
ice cubes, to serve
orange slices, to decorate

Put the mango in a blender or food processor with the orange juice and lime juice and the honey, yogurt and coconut milk.

Process until smooth, then pour the mixture over some ice cubes and serve immediately, decorated with orange slices.

maple granola

with tropical fruits and yogurt

PREP: 20 MINUTES
COOKING TIME: 5–8 MINUTES
SERVES: 6

2 tablespoons olive oil
2 tablespoons maple syrup
40 g (1½ oz) flaked almonds
40 g (1½ oz) pine nuts
25 g (1 oz) sunflower seeds
25 g (1 oz) porridge oats
375 g (12 oz) low-fat natural
   yogurt

Fruit salad
1 mango, deseeded, peeled and
   sliced
2 kiwifruit, peeled and sliced
small bunch of red seedless
   grapes, halved
grated rind and juice of 1 lime

Homemade granola is infinitely superior to the sugary, shop-bought versions. Use this wonderfully crunchy topping to enhance a tropical fruit salad and serve with spoonfuls of mild, creamy yogurt or crème fraîche.

Heat the oil in a flameproof frying pan with a metal handle, add the maple syrup and the nuts, seeds and oats and toss together.

Transfer the pan to a preheated oven, 180°C (350°F), Gas Mark 4, and cook for 5–8 minutes, stirring once and moving the brown edges to the centre, until the mixture is evenly toasted.

Leave the mixture to cool, then pack it into a storage jar. Seal, label and use within 10 days.

Make the fruit salad. Mix the fruits with the lime rind and juice, spoon the mixture into dishes and top with spoonfuls of yogurt and granola.

melon trio

with green tea infusion

PREP: 15 MINUTES, PLUS CHILLING
NO COOK
SERVES: 6

2 orange-flavoured green teabags

1 orange-fleshed melon, such as
    cantaloupe or charentais

½ green-fleshed melon, such as
    galia or ogen

½ honeydew melon

2 tablespoons light cane sugar

grated rind and juice of 1 lime

To decorate

lime wedges

6 fresh lychees

Green tea is known for its soothing, relaxing properties, and its delicate flavour perfectly complements the light perfume and freshness of the different melons.

Put the teabags into a jug and pour over 300 ml (½ pint) boiling water. Leave to infuse for 2 minutes. Lift out the bags, draining them well. Break open one of the bags, remove a few leaves and add them to the infusion. Leave to cool.

Halve the whole melon and scoop out the seeds. Remove the seeds from the other melons. Cut away the skin with a small knife and cut the orange- and green-fleshed melons into long, thin slices. Dice the honeydew melon. Put all the prepared melon into a large, shallow dish.

Sprinkle the sugar, lime rind and juice over the melon and pour over the tea. Cover with clingfilm and chill for 1 hour, or overnight if preferred.

Arrange the melon slices in fan shapes on individual serving plates. Spoon the diced melon to the side of the melon fans and serve with lime wedges and a partially peeled lychee.

muesli
energy booster

PREP: 5 MINUTES, PLUS SOAKING
NO COOK
SERVES: 1

2 tablespoons porridge oats

2 tablespoons raisins or sultanas

4 tablespoons apple or pineapple
  juice

1 apple or pear, peeled

1 tablespoon chopped mixed
  nuts

½ teaspoon ground ginger

1 teaspoon clear honey (optional)

2 tablespoons natural yogurt

This is a truly delicious breakfast, and you can make any number of variations by adding different fruits according to the season.

Soak the oats and raisins or sultanas overnight in the juice.

Next morning grate the apple or pear and mix into the oats together with the mixed nuts and ginger and, if you have a sweet tooth, the honey. Pour the yogurt on top.

stuffed figs

PREP: 5 MINUTES
NO COOK
SERVES: 1

3 ripe figs
1 tablespoon ground almonds
25 g (1 oz) raspberries
1 teaspoon clear honey
natural yogurt, to serve (optional)

Remove the stalks from the figs, make a criss-cross cut at the stalk end and carefully ease them open.

Mix together the almonds, raspberries and honey and spoon into the open figs. You can serve this with a side dish of natural yogurt, if liked.

seedy yogurt

PREP: 5 MINUTES
NO COOK
SERVES: 1

25 g (1 oz) pumpkin, sesame and
    sunflower seeds, toasted or
    ground
100 ml (3½ fl oz) natural yogurt
1 teaspoon clear honey (optional)

Stir the seeds into the yogurt. If liked, add a teaspoon of honey to make it sweeter.

smoked salmon

with scrambled eggs

PREP: 5 MINUTES
COOKING TIME: 3–4 MINUTES
SERVES: 1

15 g (½ oz) butter

3 large eggs

1 tablespoon milk

1 tablespoon cream (optional)

25–40 g (1–1½ oz) smoked
  salmon, cut into narrow strips

1 teaspoon finely snipped chives

1–2 slices warm buttered toast

salt and pepper

This is an ideal dish for a weekend brunch, but it must always be cooked just before eating.

Melt the butter in a saucepan over a gentle heat until foaming.

Break the eggs into a bowl and mix well with a fork. Add the milk and season to taste with salt and pepper.

Pour the egg mixture into the foaming butter. Stir continually with a wooden spoon, scraping the bottom of the pan and bringing the eggs from the outside to the middle. The eggs are done when they form soft, creamy curds and are barely set.

Remove the pan from the heat, stir in the cream (if used), salmon and chives and pile on to the hot toast on a warm serving plate. Serve immediately.

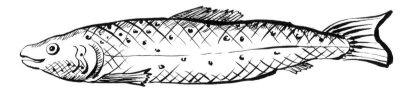

kipper kedgeree

PREP: 15 MINUTES
COOKING TIME: 20 MINUTES
SERVES: 4

250 g (8 oz) basmati rice
625 g (1¼ lb) kippers
2 teaspoons fennel seeds
8 cardamom pods
4 hard-boiled eggs
65 g (2½ oz) butter
1 onion, finely chopped
1 teaspoon ground turmeric
1 cinnamon stick
4 tablespoons chopped parsley
salt and pepper
lemon or lime wedges, to serve

Although it is usually made with smoked haddock, kedgeree adapts well to almost any smoked fish, so look out for the best deal when you are shopping.

Cook the rice in plenty of boiling water for about 10 minutes or until tender. Drain.

Meanwhile, put the kippers in a frying pan, just cover with hot water and simmer gently for 5 minutes. Drain. When the fish is cool enough to handle, roughly flake the flesh, discarding the skin and bones.

Crush the fennel seeds and cardamom pods using a pestle and mortar. Remove the cardamom pods, leaving the seeds. Shell and quarter the eggs.

Melt half the butter in a frying pan and gently fry the onion and all the spices for 5 minutes. Stir in the rice, fish, eggs and parsley and season to taste with salt and pepper. Serve with lemon or lime wedges.

buckwheat
pancakes

PREP: 10 MINUTES, PLUS
STANDING
COOKING TIME: 15 MINUTES
MAKES: 12–15 PANCAKES

125 g (4 oz) buckwheat flour
3 eggs
300 ml (½ pint) milk
2 tablespoons groundnut oil
salt

These pancakes can be served with sweet or savoury toppings. They are excellent with bacon or sausage and delicious with honey and lemon.

Make the batter. Sift the flour and a pinch of salt into a bowl. Make a well in the centre, add the eggs and beat well. Add half the milk and the oil and beat to a smooth batter. Cover and leave to stand for 2 hours.

Lightly oil a 20 cm (8 inch) frying pan and place over a moderate heat, until the oil just begins to smoke. Add about 2 tablespoons of the batter or enough for a thin, even coating of the pan when it is tilted. Cook until the batter has set and is lightly golden at the edges.

Toss the pancake and cook for 20–30 seconds or until golden on the second side. Remove the pan from the heat and slide the pancake on to a warm plate. Cover with a tea towel and keep warm. Repeat with the remaining batter.

Fold each pancake in half and then in half again. Serve with a topping of your choice.

gravlax

with cream cheese and chives

PREP: 15 MINUTES
COOKING TIME: 14–16 MINUTES
SERVES: 2

2 poppy and sesame seed
    bagels, cut in half horizontally
125 g (4 oz) cream cheese
175 g (6 oz) gravlax, finely sliced
2 tablespoons snipped chives

Hollandaise sauce
2 tablespoons white wine vinegar
1 bay leaf
½ teaspoon black peppercorns
3 egg yolks
200 g (7 oz) unsalted butter,
    softened and cut into 1 cm
    (½ inch) cubes
salt and pepper

Make the sauce. Put the vinegar, bay leaf, peppercorns and 1 tablespoon water in a small saucepan. Heat until bubbling and simmer until the liquid has reduced by half.

Put the egg yolks in a heatproof bowl that sits comfortably over a pan of simmering water without the base touching the water. Strain the vinegar mixture into the yolks and whisk to combine.

Whisk in a cube of butter. As soon as it has melted into the sauce, add another cube and whisk until it is absorbed. Continue adding butter, a cube at a time, until the sauce is thick and glossy. Check the flavour, season with salt and pepper and keep warm.

Put the bagels, cut side down, on a sandwich grill. Do not close the lid. Leave them to toast for 2–3 minutes then remove from the grill. Spread the bases with cream cheese and top with gravlax. Scatter over the snipped chives and season with black pepper.

Top the bagels with the lids and return them to the sandwich grill. Lower the top plate and toast for 2–3 minutes or according to the manufacturer's instructions, until golden and crispy. Serve immediately with a spoonful of warm sauce and a sprinkling of black pepper.

french toast

with honey and lemon

PREP: 10 MINUTES, PLUS COOLING
AND STANDING
COOKING TIME: 15–20 MINUTES
SERVES: 4

300 ml (½ pint) milk

100 g (3½ oz) clear honey, plus
    extra to serve

2 strips of lemon rind

pinch of ground cinnamon

8 large slices of day-old bread,
    crusts removed

vegetable oil, for frying

2 eggs, beaten

To serve

peeled orange slices

lemon wedges

This is a sweet version of the original French toast –
a brunch favourite – which the Spanish serve as a
breakfast dish.

Warm the milk, honey, lemon rind and cinnamon in a heavy-based
saucepan until almost boiling. Remove from the heat and leave to cool
for 20 minutes.

Cut the bread slices in half diagonally to make triangles and dip each
piece into the infused milk. Transfer the slices to a wire rack set over a
tray and allow to dry for 2 hours.

Heat a shallow layer of oil in a large frying pan. Dip the bread triangles
into the beaten eggs and fry for 1–2 minutes on each side or until they
are golden.

Serve the toast with a drizzle of honey, peeled orange slices and lemon
wedges for squeezing.

' When my mum was going through treatment she really craved creamy flavours, so I decided to combine two favourites and create this delicious breakfast dish. When she was particularly tired from treatment, she loved being brought this for breakfast in bed with a cup of tea. **'**

Laura Miller,
Breast Cancer Care employee,
mother diagnosed 1999

raisin
toasty treat ❀

PREP: 5 MINUTES
COOKING TIME: 5 MINUTES
SERVES: 1

raisin bread
ricotta cheese
walnut pieces
maple syrup or honey

Toast the raisin bread on both sides under a preheated grill.

Blend the ricotta with walnuts and maple syrup and spread it on the toast. If you don't have maple syrup or would prefer a slightly different flavour use honey.

portobello
mushrooms
with baked beans and grilled haloumi slices

PREP: 10 MINUTES
COOKING TIME: 20 MINUTES
SERVES: 4

4 large portobello mushrooms

2 garlic cloves, finely chopped

4 tablespoons chopped mixed
fresh herbs (such as thyme,
rosemary, chives and parsley)

6 tablespoons olive oil

415 g (13½ oz) can baked beans

few drops of balsamic vinegar

8 thin slices of haloumi cheese

pepper

To serve

75 g (3 oz) rocket leaves

1 pear, cored, peeled and sliced

25 g (1 oz) freshly grated
Parmesan cheese

Remove the stems from the mushrooms and place the caps, gill sides up, in an ovenproof dish. Sprinkle over half the garlic and herbs and season with pepper. Drizzle the mushrooms with half the oil, place in a preheated oven, 200°C (400°F), Gas Mark 6, and roast for 10–15 minutes or until cooked through.

Mix the beans with a few drops of balsamic vinegar and heat through gently. Spoon the beans over the cooked mushrooms and arrange the slices of haloumi over the beans. Scatter over the reserved garlic and herbs and drizzle with the remaining oil.

Place the dish under a preheated high grill and cook for 2–3 minutes or until the haloumi is golden-brown. Divide the dish into individual portions and serve immediately with a rocket, pear and Parmesan salad.

BLT sandwich

PREP: 5 MINUTES
COOKING TIME: 5–7 MINUTES
SERVES: 1

2 lean rashers of bacon

2 slices of wholemeal or
   multigrain bread, toasted

2 tablespoons mayonnaise

3 cherry tomatoes, halved

about 4 baby lettuce leaves

salt and pepper

For a tasty variation, use rye or white bread and place a slice of Cheddar cheese on top of the toast. Grill until bubbling and place the remaining ingredients on top, omitting the mayonnaise.

Cook the bacon in a small, nonstick frying pan until golden-brown and crisp, turning once. Remove and drain on kitchen paper.

Spread the toast with mayonnaise and arrange the bacon, tomato and lettuce on one slice. Season to taste with salt and pepper and top with the remaining slice. Serve hot or cold.

croque monsieur

PREP: 5 MINUTES
COOKING TIME: 5 MINUTES
SERVES: 2

50 g (2 oz) butter
4 slices of bread from a white
    sandwich loaf
2 slices of Gruyère cheese
2 thin slices of cooked lean ham
3 tablespoons sunflower oil
pepper

Spread half the butter over 1 side of the bread. Place a slice of cheese on 2 of the buttered slices, top with a slice of ham and season to taste with a little black pepper. Top with the remaining slices of bread, buttered sides down, pressing down firmly.

Melt the remaining butter with the oil in a frying pan and fry the croques until they are golden-brown, turning once. Serve immediately.

potato herb
scones

PREP: 20 MINUTES
COOKING TIME: 30–35 MINUTES
MAKES: 8 SCONES

375 g (12 oz) potatoes, peeled
   and cut into evenly-sized
   pieces
15 g (½ oz) butter
2 tablespoons snipped chives
2 tablespoons chopped parsley
75 g (3 oz) plain or wholemeal
   flour
a little milk (optional)
flour, for dusting
sunflower oil, for frying
salt and pepper

Cook the potatoes in a large saucepan of lightly salted boiling water for about 20 minutes or until tender.

Drain the potatoes into a bowl and mash them with the butter. Season to taste with salt and pepper and stir in the chives and parsley. Beat in the flour. Add a little milk if the mixture is dry.

Form the potato mixture into a ball and divide it into 8 pieces. Roll each one out on a lightly floured surface to a thickness of about 5 mm (¼ inch). Prick the surface all over with a fork.

Lightly oil a heavy-based frying pan. Heat the pan, then cook the potato scones, a few at a time, for 3 minutes on each side or until they are golden-brown.

cranberry, orange and vanilla
muffins

PREP: 10 MINUTES
COOKING TIME: 15–20 MINUTES
MAKES: 12 MUFFINS

150 g (5 oz) unsalted butter,
    melted
175 ml (6 fl oz) milk
1 egg
finely grated rind of 1 orange
1 teaspoon vanilla extract
375 g (12 oz) self-raising flour
2 teaspoons baking powder
125 g (4 oz) dried cranberries
50 g (2 oz) sugar
50 g (2 oz) light brown sugar

Dried blueberries or cherries make equally good alternatives to the cranberries. You could also omit the orange rind and use a teaspoon of ground cinnamon or allspice instead.

Mix together the butter, milk, egg, orange rind and vanilla extract.

Sift the flour and baking powder into a bowl and stir in the cranberries and the sugars. Add the milk mixture to the bowl and stir briefly until only just combined.

Line a 12-section muffin tin with paper cases. Spoon the mixture into the paper cases, piling it up in the centre.

Bake the muffins in a preheated oven, 190°C (375°F), Gas Mark 5, for 15–20 minutes or until they are well risen and golden-brown. Transfer them to a wire rack to cool slightly and serve warm.

dark orange and lemon
marmalade

PREP: 30 MINUTES, PLUS
STANDING
COOKING TIME: 2 HOURS
MAKES: ABOUT 2 KG (4 LB)

2 large oranges, finely chopped
    and pips discarded
4 large lemons, finely chopped
    and pips discarded
1 kg (2 lb) sugar
250 g (8 oz) muscovado sugar

A small amount of muscovado sugar gives this marmalade a good, rich flavour. For a tangy flavour use Seville oranges when they are in season.

Put the fruit in a large saucepan and add 1.8 litres (3 pints) water. Bring to the boil, then reduce the heat, cover the pan and simmer for 1½ hours.

Add all the sugar to the pan and cook over a low heat, stirring continuously, until the sugar has completely dissolved. Increase the heat and bring to a rolling boil, then boil hard to setting point. Use a slotted spoon skim off any scum, then leave the marmalade to stand for 15 minutes to allow the fruit to settle.

Stir the marmalade and transfer to warm, dry jars. Cover the surface of each one with a disc of waxed paper, waxed side down, then leave until cold. Top the cold jars with airtight lids or cellophane covers. Label and store in a cool, dark place. The marmalade will keep for 3–4 months.

meals in bowls

All these recipes are the ultimate in comfort food, with wonderfully fresh ingredients combined with warming spices to create delicious soups, curries and casseroles. You'll find classics such as *Celery and Stilton Soup*, as well as more unusual dishes like the fragrant *Chicken with Lemon Grass and Asparagus.*

prawn and kaffir lime
soup

PREP: 15 MINUTES
COOKING TIME: 20 MINUTES
SERVES: 4

5 red Thai chillies

6 kaffir lime leaves

1 string of green peppercorns

1 lemon grass stalk, finely sliced

2 tablespoons Thai fish sauce

2 tablespoons sugar

500 g (1 lb) raw large prawns,
   shelled and deveined

4 tablespoons lime or lemon juice

handful of coriander leaves

boiled rice, to serve

This simple Thai soup contains large prawns and kaffir lime leaves. Strings of green peppercorns can be found in Asian grocery stores; they add a peppery flavour but are not eaten. If you cannot get them, use peppercorns in brine instead.

Put the chillies, kaffir lime leaves, peppercorns and lemon grass into a large, heavy-based saucepan and add 1.2 litres (2 pints) water. Bring gently to the boil and simmer for 10 minutes. Reduce the heat and add the fish sauce and sugar.

When the liquid is simmering, add the prawns and simmer gently until they have turned pink. Remove the pan from the heat and add the lime juice and coriander leaves. Serve the soup immediately with plain boiled rice.

$\mathcal{R}$ick Stein's
steamed mussels with tomato and tarragon

PREP: 12 MINUTES
COOKING TIME: 8 MINUTES
SERVES: 2–4

2 tablespoons extra virgin
    olive oil
2 garlic cloves, finely chopped
1 kg (2 lb) mussels or pippies
2 tablespoons dry white wine
25 g (1 oz) unsalted butter
2 tomatoes, peeled, deseeded
    and finely chopped
2 teaspoons French tarragon,
    finely chopped
salt and pepper
crusty bread or pasta, to serve

Heat the oil in a large, heavy-based saucepan and soften the garlic over a medium heat for about a minute. Add the mussels or pippies, turn up the heat and add the white wine. Cover the pan and cook for a few minutes until all the shells have opened but only just. Stir the shells once or twice during the cooking to distribute them evenly. Remove the pan from the heat and pour the mussels through a colander set over a bowl. Discard any that have not opened during cooking.

Keep the mussels warm while you transfer the liquor to a pan. Heat until boiling. Whisk in the butter then add the tomatoes and tarragon. Check the seasoning. (It's a good idea to leave seasoning to the end with shellfish because you never know how salty they are going to be, then add salt if necessary and freshly ground black pepper.)

Add the mussels to the pan. Serve with plenty of crusty bread or with a mound of *al dente* linguine pasta.

cauliflower cheese
soup

PREP: 15–20 MINUTES
COOKING TIME: 1¼ HOURS
SERVES: 6

2 tablespoons vegetable oil

1 onion, finely chopped

1 large cauliflower, about 1.2 kg
   (2½ lb), cut into florets

50 g (2 oz) strong Cheddar
   cheese, grated

pepper

Vegetable stock

500 g (1 lb) mixed vegetables
   (excluding potatoes, parsnips
   and other starchy root
   vegetables), chopped

1 garlic clove, thinly sliced

6 peppercorns

1 bouquet garni

To serve

2 tablespoons pumpkin seeds

4 tablespoons reduced-fat
   fromage frais

Make the vegetable stock. Put all the ingredients plus 1.2 litres (2 pints) water into a large, heavy-based saucepan. Bring to the boil and simmer gently for 30 minutes, skimming if necessary. Strain the stock through a muslin-lined sieve, return it to the saucepan and keep warm. These ingredients will make about 1 litre (1¾ pints), and any stock not used in this recipe can be chilled then frozen for use in other dishes.

Meanwhile, heat the oil in a large saucepan, add the onion and cook gently until it is soft but not browned. Add the cauliflower florets, cover and cook for 5–10 minutes. Stir in 900 ml (1½ pints) of the vegetable stock and simmer for 30 minutes until the cauliflower is tender.

Lightly toast the pumpkin seeds in a dry, nonstick frying pan. They will start to pop when they are ready, but keep watch while they cook because they can easily burn.

Purée the soup in a food processor or rub through a sieve and return it to the saucepan. Add the Cheddar and season to taste with pepper. Reheat thoroughly, without boiling, until the cheese melts through the soup. If necessary, thin the soup by adding more liquid, such as hot stock or vegetable water.

Serve in warm bowls with a swirl of fromage frais and a sprinkling of toasted pumpkin seeds.

celery and stilton
soup ❋

PREP: 10 MINUTES
COOKING TIME: 40 MINUTES
SERVES: 4–5

50 g (2 oz) butter
2 onions, roughly chopped
1 garlic clove, chopped
2 celery hearts, about 700 g
   (1 lb 6 oz), chopped
1 litre (1¾ pints) stock, or
   4 teaspoons of bouillon
   powder dissolved in 1 litre
   (1¾ pints) water
125 g (4 oz) Stilton cheese,
   crumbled
pepper

Melt the butter in a deep frying pan with a lid, add the onions and cook over a low heat for about 5 minutes. Add the garlic and celery and cook for 5 minutes more.

Add the stock, bring to a simmer and cook for about 30 minutes or until the celery is tender. Add the Stilton and allow to melt.

Allow the soup to cool a little then blend, in batches if necessary, in a food processor or with a stick blender until the soup has a chunky consistency. Season with pepper and reheat gently, but do not allow to boil, before serving.

' This soup is special to me because I love Stilton. After I had finished chemotherapy and my taste returned to normal, I made this soup as a special treat. It was heaven! '
Suzanne Price, diagnosed 2006

minestrone soup

PREP: 5 MINUTES
COOKING TIME: 25 MINUTES
SERVES: 4

2 tablespoons olive oil

1 onion, chopped

1 garlic clove, crushed

2 celery sticks, chopped

1 leek, finely sliced

1 carrot, chopped

400 g (13 oz) can chopped
   tomatoes

600 ml (1 pint) chicken or
   vegetable stock

1 courgette, diced

½ small cabbage, shredded

1 bay leaf

75 g (3 oz) can haricot beans,
   drained

75 g (3 oz) dried spaghetti,
   broken into small pieces, or
   small pasta shapes

1 tablespoon chopped flat leaf
   parsley

salt and pepper

50 g (2 oz) Parmesan cheese,
   freshly grated, to serve

Heat the oil in a large, heavy-based saucepan. Add the onion, garlic, celery, leek and carrot and cook over a medium heat, stirring occasionally, for about 3 minutes.

Add the tomatoes, stock, courgette, cabbage, bay leaf and beans. Bring to the boil, then reduce the heat and simmer for 10 minutes.

Add the pasta and season to taste with salt and pepper. Stir well and cook for a further 8 minutes. Keep stirring because the soup may stick to the base of the pan. Just before serving, add the parsley and mix well. Ladle the soup into warm bowls and serve with grated Parmesan.

gazpacho

PREP: 15 MINUTES, PLUS CHILLING
NO COOK
SERVES: 6

2 garlic cloves, roughly chopped

¼ teaspoon salt

3 thick slices of white bread,
   crusts removed

1 kg (2 lb) tomatoes, skinned and
   roughly chopped

2 onions, roughly chopped

½ large cucumber, peeled,
   deseeded and roughly
   chopped

2 large green peppers, cored,
   deseeded and roughly
   chopped

5 tablespoons olive oil

4 tablespoons white wine vinegar

pepper

small ice cubes, to serve

Combine the garlic and salt in a mortar and pound with a pestle until smooth. Put the bread in a bowl, cover with cold water and leave to soak for 5 seconds. Drain the bread, then squeeze out the moisture.

Set aside a quarter of the tomatoes, onions, cucumber and green peppers for garnishing. Put the remaining vegetables in a food processor. Add the garlic paste, bread and oil and process until smooth.

Pour the mixture into a bowl and stir in the vinegar and 1 litre (1¾ pints) iced water. Season to taste with pepper, cover and place in the freezer for 15 minutes.

Meanwhile, finely chop the reserved vegetables. Serve the soup in chilled bowls, adding 2–3 ice cubes to each bowl and topping the soup with the chopped vegetables.

beef and noodle
broth

PREP: 15 MINUTES
COOKING TIME: 10 MINUTES
SERVES: 2

300 g (10 oz) rump or sirloin steak
15 g (½ oz) fresh root ginger,
    peeled and grated
2 teaspoons soy sauce
50 g (2 oz) vermicelli rice noodles
600 ml (1 pint) beef or chicken
    stock
1 red chilli, deseeded and finely
    chopped
1 garlic clove, thinly sliced
2 teaspoons caster sugar
2 teaspoons vegetable oil
75 g (3 oz) mangetout, halved
    lengthways
small handful of Thai basil, torn
    into pieces

This quick and easy soup relies on good-quality, well-flavoured stock and is ideal for using up any beef or chicken stock that you might have in the freezer. When slicing the beef, use a sharp knife and cut it across the grain so that it falls into tender, succulent slices.

Trim any fat from the beef. Mix the ginger with 1 teaspoon soy sauce and smooth over both sides of the beef.

Cook the noodles according to the directions on the packet. Drain and rinse thoroughly in cold water.

Put the stock in a large, heavy-based saucepan, add the chilli, garlic and sugar and bring to a gentle simmer. Cover and cook gently for 5 minutes.

Heat the oil in a nonstick frying pan and fry the beef for 2 minutes on each side. Transfer the meat to a board, cut it in half lengthways and then cut it across into thin strips.

Add the noodles, mangetout, basil and remaining soy sauce to the soup and heat gently for 1 minute. Stir in the beef and serve immediately.

> ❛ This recipe comes from my ancestors, and I was told it was "Jewish penicillin". At my very worst during treatment this would be the only food I could stomach. The soup isn't too thick, but it's very warming and tasty. It has to be the simplest of dishes to make, and without fail it would make me feel so much better. ❜
>
> **Sharon Eglash**, diagnosed 2002, mother diagnosed 1999

traditional chicken
soup ✸

PREP: 10 MINUTES
COOKING TIME: 1 HOUR
SERVES: 2–3

2 stock cubes or 1 litre (1¾ pints)
   organic chicken stock
4 organic chicken drumsticks or
   thighs
2 carrots, sliced
2 celery sticks, sliced
2 tablespoons pearl barley
handful of vermicelli noodles,
   about 50 g (2 oz)

Crumble the stock cubes into 1 litre (1¾ pints) of cold water in a large, heavy-based saucepan (or pour in the stock if using). Add the chicken, carrots, celery and barley and bring to a simmer. Cover and cook gently for 45 minutes until the chicken is tender.

Remove the chicken pieces and, when they are cool enough to handle, shred the chicken, discarding the skin and bones. Return the meat to the pan, add the noodles and cook gently for 10 minutes before serving.

garganelli

with roasted cherry tomatoes

PREP: 15 MINUTES, PLUS CHILLING
COOKING TIME: 40 MINUTES
SERVES: 4–6

200 g (7 oz) cherry tomatoes,
   halved
2 teaspoons chopped thyme
½ teaspoon caster sugar
150 ml (¼ pint) olive oil
200 g (7 oz) fresh or dried
   garganelli
2 teaspoons coriander seeds
1 teaspoon mustard seeds
25 g (1 oz) chopped herbs, such
   as chervil, tarragon, flat leaf
   parsley or chives
1 garlic clove, crushed
finely grated rind of 1 lime, plus
   2 tablespoons juice
3 tablespoons capers, drained
   and rinsed
salt and pepper

This fresh, summery salad is tossed in a herby,
Mediterranean-style sauce, which is delicious with the
roasted tomatoes.

Arrange the tomatoes, cut sides up, in a single layer in a roasting tin.
Sprinkle with the thyme, sugar, 2 tablespoons of the oil and a little salt
and pepper. Roast in a preheated oven, 200°C (400°F), Gas Mark 6,
for about 40 minutes or until the tomatoes are soft and browned
around the edges.

Meanwhile, bring a large saucepan of lightly salted water to the boil.
Add the pasta, return to the boil and cook, allowing 3 minutes for fresh
pasta and 8–10 minutes for dried. Drain the pasta and toss in a bowl
with 1 tablespoon oil.

Use a pestle and mortar to crush the coriander and mustard seeds.
Tip them into a small saucepan with the remaining oil, herbs, garlic, lime
rind and juice and a little salt and pepper and warm through gently for
2–3 minutes for the flavours to mingle.

Scatter the roasted tomatoes and the capers over the pasta and pour
over the dressing. Toss the salad together and chill until ready to serve.

spiced vegetable
semolina

PREP: 15 MINUTES
COOKING TIME: ABOUT
25 MINUTES
SERVES: 4

175 g (6 oz) coarse semolina
1 tablespoon sunflower oil
1 teaspoon black mustard seeds
1 teaspoon cumin seeds
1 dried red chilli
10–12 curry leaves
1 onion, finely chopped
1 teaspoon garam masala
1 carrot, finely diced
100 g (3½ oz) fresh or frozen peas
10–12 cherry tomatoes, halved
salt
freshly chopped coriander leaves,
    to garnish
lemon wedges, to serve

This hearty Indian dish, known as *uppama*, is rather like a pilaf. It comes from the southwestern state of Kerala, where there are many variations using different combinations of spices and vegetables. Mustard seeds are a traditional flavouring.

Put the semolina in a large, nonstick frying pan and dry-roast it over a medium heat for 8–10 minutes or until golden-brown. Remove the semolina from the pan and set aside.

Return the pan to the heat and add the oil. When it is hot, add the mustard seeds, cumin seeds, chilli, curry leaves and onion. Stir-fry over a medium heat for 5–6 minutes or until the onion has softened, then add the garam masala, carrot, peas and cherry tomatoes and stir-fry for 1–2 minutes.

Add the semolina and 600 ml (1 pint) boiling water. Stir and cook for 5–6 minutes over a low heat or until the semolina has absorbed all the water. Season to taste with salt and garnish with chopped coriander then serve with wedges of lemon.

Rose Elliot's
laksa

" This Malaysian soup–stew is light but filling, and I find the spices have a really uplifting effect on energy and morale. For a pure vegetarian version use Thai paste that does not contain shrimp paste – there is a supermarket own-brand one that is suitable. "

PREP: 15 MINUTES
COOKING TIME: 20 MINUTES
SERVES: 4

125 g (4 oz) rice noodles
2 tablespoons oil
1 tablespoon vegetarian Thai
  paste
250 g (8 oz) shiitake mushrooms,
  sliced
1 red chilli, deseeded and sliced
400 ml (14 fl oz) can coconut milk
1 aubergine
2 pak choi, trimmed and halved
125 g (4 oz) baby sweetcorn,
  halved diagonally
20 g (¾ oz) fresh coriander,
  roughly chopped
salt and pepper

Put the rice noodles in a bowl and cover with boiling water. Leave to soak for 5–10 minutes, then drain.

Heat 1 tablespoon oil in a large saucepan, add the Thai paste and let it sizzle for a few seconds until it is aromatic, then add the mushrooms and chilli. Stir, then pour in the coconut milk and 400 ml (14 fl oz) water. Reduce the heat and leave the soup to simmer for 10–15 minutes.

Meanwhile, cut the aubergine into 7 mm (⅛ inch) slices. Brush both sides of each slice with the rest of the oil and grill for about 7 minutes on each side until tender and lightly browned. Set aside to cool, then cut into dice.

Cook the pak choi in boiling water for about 6 minutes or until tender. Drain well.

Add the noodles, aubergine, pak choi and sweetcorn to the coconut mixture, bring the mixture to the boil and simmer gently for 1–2 minutes to heat everything through and cook the sweetcorn.

Season the laksa to taste with salt and pepper, ladle it into warm bowls and serve topped with chopped coriander.

chicken

with lemon grass and asparagus

PREP: 10 MINUTES
COOKING TIME: ABOUT
15 MINUTES
SERVES: 4

1 tablespoon rapeseed or olive oil

2 garlic cloves, crushed

2 tablespoons finely chopped
  lemon grass

2 teaspoons finely chopped fresh
  root ginger

1 onion, sliced

500 g (1 lb) boneless, skinless
  chicken breast, cut into strips

300 g (10 oz) vine-ripened
  tomatoes, chopped

350 g (12 oz) asparagus spears,
  halved length- and widthways

1 tablespoon shoyu or tamari
  sauce

½ teaspoon ground black pepper

handful of Thai basil leaves, to
  garnish

This dish has a Thai influence, with lots of lemon grass, ginger and basil leaves. The addition of vine-ripened tomatoes moistens the dish and lends a taste of the Mediterranean.

Heat the oil in a large, nonstick frying pan over a high heat until it is hot, swirling the oil around the pan.

Add the garlic, lemon grass, ginger and onion and stir-fry for about 5 minutes.

Add the chicken and stir-fry for 5–7 minutes or until the chicken is browned and cooked through.

Add the tomatoes, asparagus, shoyu or tamari sauce and pepper and stir-fry for 2–3 minutes to warm through. Garnish with the Thai basil leaves and serve immediately.

ginger chicken

with honey

PREP: 15 MINUTES, PLUS SOAKING
COOKING TIME: 10–15 MINUTES
SERVES: 4

50 g (2 oz) fresh root ginger,
   peeled and finely chopped

2 tablespoons vegetable oil

3 boneless, skinless chicken
   breasts, chopped

3 chicken livers, chopped

1 onion, thinly sliced

3 garlic cloves, crushed

2 tablespoons dried black fungus,
   soaked in hot water for
   20 minutes

2 tablespoons soy sauce

1 tablespoon clear honey

5 spring onions, chopped

1 fresh red chilli, deseeded
   and thinly sliced into strips,
   to garnish

rice sticks, to serve (optional)

Mix the ginger with a little cold water, then drain and squeeze it dry. Set aside.

Heat the oil in a wok or large, nonstick frying pan and add the chicken breasts and livers. Stir-fry the meat over a moderate heat for 5 minutes, then remove it with a slotted spoon and set aside.

Add the onion to the wok or frying pan and cook gently until soft, then add the garlic and the drained black fungus and stir-fry for 1 minute. Return the chicken mixture to the wok and stir to combine.

Mix together the soy sauce and honey in a bowl until blended, then pour this into the wok and stir well. Add the drained ginger and stir-fry for 2–3 minutes. Finally, add the spring onions. Serve immediately, garnished with strips of red chilli and accompanied by rice sticks, if liked.

stir-fried duck

with mango

PREP: 15 MINUTES, PLUS
MARINATING
COOKING TIME: ABOUT
15 MINUTES
SERVES: 2

1 large boneless, skinless duck
   breast
1 ripe mango
4 tablespoons groundnut oil
1 large fresh red chilli, deseeded
   and thinly sliced
75 g (3 oz) Chinese leaves or
   Savoy cabbage, shredded

Marinade
2 tablespoons light or dark soy
   sauce
1 tablespoon rice wine vinegar or
   white wine vinegar
½ teaspoon chilli oil
2.5 cm (1 inch) fresh root ginger,
   peeled and grated
½ teaspoon Chinese five spice
   powder

Cut the duck flesh into thin strips, cutting diagonally against the grain. Transfer the meat to a non-metallic dish. Make the marinade by mixing together all the ingredients, pour it into the dish with the duck and stir to mix. Cover the dish and leave to marinate at room temperature for about 30 minutes.

Meanwhile, cut the mango lengthways into 3 pieces, avoiding the stone. Peel the pieces of mango and cut the flesh into strips about the same size as the duck.

Heat half the oil in a wok or large, nonstick frying pan. Add half the duck strips and stir-fry over a high heat for 4–5 minutes or until the meat is just tender. Remove the duck with a slotted spoon and repeat with the remaining oil and duck.

Return all of the duck to the wok or frying pan and sprinkle with the chilli. Toss to mix, then add the mango and Chinese leaves or cabbage and toss for 1–2 minutes or until the leaves start to wilt. Serve immediately.

cassoulet

PREP: 30 MINUTES, PLUS SOAKING
COOKING TIME: ABOUT 3½ HOURS
SERVES: 6

625 g (1¼ lb) dried haricot beans, soaked overnight in water

4 tablespoons olive oil or goose fat

750 g (1½ lb) piece belly pork, skinned and cut into chunks

4 duck legs, halved

8 garlicky sausages

2 onions, chopped

2 bay leaves

1.2 litres (2 pints) chicken stock

4 garlic cloves, crushed

good pinch of ground cloves

3 tablespoons tomato paste

75 g (3 oz) breadcrumbs

salt and pepper

In a good cassoulet the beans turn soft and creamy and thicken the meaty juices. For convenience, use fresh duck, but if you have more time use duck confit.

Drain the beans and put them in a large saucepan. Cover them with cold water, bring to the boil and boil rapidly for 10 minutes. Reduce the heat and simmer gently for 30 minutes until slightly softened. Drain.

Heat the oil or fat in a large, heavy-based frying pan. Fry the pork pieces, in batches, until the meat is lightly browned, then lift out and drain. Fry the duck pieces and sausages until browned.

Tip half the beans into a large earthenware pot or casserole dish and scatter over half the meat, half the chopped onions and the bay leaves. Add the remaining beans, meat and onions.

Blend the stock with the garlic, cloves and tomato paste and pour the mixture over the beans. Season to taste with salt and pepper and top up with a little water so that the beans are nearly submerged. Cover and cook in a preheated oven, 160°C (325°F), Gas Mark 3, for 2 hours until the beans are completely tender.

Scatter the breadcrumbs over the surface and return the cassoulet to the oven, uncovered, for a further 30–40 minutes until golden.

sweet and sour
pork

PREP: 20 MINUTES
COOKING TIME: ABOUT
10 MINUTES
SERVES: 4

1 egg white, slightly beaten

1 teaspoon black pepper

500 g (1 lb) pork fillet or loin, cut
 into 1 cm (½ inch) thick slices

4 tablespoons cornflour

1 tablespoon rapeseed or olive oil

Sweet and sour sauce

5 teaspoons cornflour

5 tablespoons stock or water

3 tablespoons tomato ketchup

1 teaspoon white wine vinegar

200 g (7 oz) fresh tomatoes,
 roughly chopped

4 tablespoons pineapple juice

2 teaspoons sugar

150 g (5 oz) pineapple pieces

150 g (5 oz) green pepper, cored,
 deseeded and cut into 2.5 cm
 (1 inch) squares

125 g (4 oz) onion, cut into 2.5 cm
 (1 inch) squares

This Cantonese dish is extremely popular in Chinese takeaways and restaurants. This recipe uses lean pork rather than the traditional belly pork for a healthier alternative. Re-create your own takeaway menu by serving this with *Special Egg-fried Rice* (see page 51).

Mix together the egg white and pepper and rub it into the pork slices. Dip each piece of pork into the cornflour, shaking off the excess.

Heat the oil in a wok or large, nonstick frying pan over a high heat. Put the pork slices into the wok or pan, making sure there is a little space between each one, and fry for 2 minutes on each side. Turn down the heat to medium and stir-fry the pork for another 2 minutes or until cooked through. Transfer to a serving plate and keep warm.

Make the sweet and sour sauce. Mix the cornflour with the stock or water to make a smooth paste and combine it with all the ingredients in a small saucepan. Add 200 ml (7 fl oz) water and bring to the boil.

Pour the sauce over the pork and serve immediately.

special
egg-fried rice

PREP: 10 MINUTES
COOKING TIME: 10–12 MINUTES
SERVES: 4

2–3 eggs

2 spring onions, finely chopped,
plus extra to garnish

2 teaspoons salt

3 tablespoons vegetable oil

125 g (4 oz) cooked peeled
prawns

125 g (4 oz) cooked chicken or
pork, diced

50 g (2 oz) bamboo shoots,
roughly chopped

4 tablespoons fresh or frozen
peas, cooked

1 tablespoon light soy sauce

375–500 g (12 oz–1 lb) cold
cooked rice

Break the eggs into a small bowl and add 1 teaspoon of the spring onions and a pinch of the salt. Beat lightly together with a fork to combine.

Heat about 1 tablespoon oil in a wok or large, nonstick frying pan and add the beaten egg mixture. Stir constantly until the eggs are scrambled and set. Remove the eggs from the wok and set aside in a bowl.

Heat the remaining oil in the wok or frying pan and add the prawns, meat, bamboo shoots, peas and the rest of the spring onions. Stir-fry briskly for 1 minute, then stir in the soy sauce. Stir-fry for 2–3 minutes.

Add the cooked rice with the eggs and remaining salt. Stir well to break up the eggs into small pieces and to separate the grains of rice.

Denise Welch's
red stew

' As my mother had surgery for cancer of the soft palate
16 years ago, I am always eager to help any cancer-related
charities. This recipe was always one of my favourite meals
when I was young and has continued to be one I regularly
use – and, of course, I always think of my mother when I use
it and how fortunate I am that she is still with us. '

PREP: 25 MINUTES
COOKING TIME: 3 HOURS
SERVES: 6–8

1 tablespoons vegetable oil

1 large onion, chopped

2 beef stock cubes

1 kg (2 lb) stewing or braising
   beef, cubed

340 g (11½ oz) can corned beef,
   roughly chopped

2 large carrots, chopped

400 g (13 oz) can chopped
   tomatoes

2 tablespoons tomato purée

125 g (4 oz) frozen peas

125 g (4 oz) sweetcorn

420 g (13½ oz) can baked beans

2 teaspoons cornflour (optional)

salt and pepper

crusty or garlic bread, to serve

Heat the oil in a frying pan and gently cook the onion for 5 minutes. Transfer the onion to a casserole dish.

Crumble the stock cubes into 600 ml (1 pint) water and add, with the beef and corned beef, to the casserole dish. Cover and cook in a preheated oven, 160°C (325°F), Gas Mark 3, for 1½ hours.

Add the carrots, tomatoes and tomato purée to the casserole and return to the oven for a further hour or until the carrots are tender.

Put the peas, sweetcorn and beans into the dish. If necessary, thicken the sauce by mixing the cornflour with 2 teaspoons water. Season with salt and pepper and return to the oven for 15 minutes more. Serve with crusty or garlic bread.

indian lamb

with almond sauce

PREP: 25 MINUTES
COOKING TIME: 1¼ HOURS
SERVES: 5–6

750 g (1½ lb) lamb neck fillet
10 whole cardamom pods
1 tablespoon cumin seeds
3 tablespoons vegetable oil
1 hot red chilli, deseeded and
  chopped
1 tablespoon desiccated coconut
50 g (2 oz) blanched almonds,
  chopped
40 g (1½ oz) fresh root ginger,
  grated
4 garlic cloves, chopped
1 teaspoon ground turmeric
1 onion, finely chopped
4 tablespoons natural yogurt
500 g (1 lb) tomatoes, skinned
  and chopped
salt
rice, to serve

This recipe is like a quick and easy *roghan josh* with chunks of tender lamb in a richly spiced, nutty sauce. Like many spiced meat dishes, this reheats well.

Cut the lamb into chunks, discarding any fat, and pat dry. Crush the cardamom and cumin seeds. Heat the oil in a large, heavy-based frying pan and gently fry the chilli, cardamom and cumin.

Add half the lamb and fry, stirring, until well browned. Lift out with a slotted spoon and transfer the meat to a large saucepan. Fry the remaining lamb and add it to the pan.

Add the coconut and almonds to the frying pan and fry until lightly browned. Tip into a blender or food processor with the ginger, garlic, turmeric, onion and 6 tablespoons water and blend to a paste. Return to the frying pan, add the yogurt and cook, stirring, for 5 minutes.

Stir in another 150 ml (¼ pint) water and pour over the lamb. Add the tomatoes. Cover and cook on the lowest heat for about 1 hour or until the lamb is tender. Season to taste with salt and serve with rice.

beef kofta curry

PREP: 20 MINUTES
COOKING TIME: 15–20 MINUTES
SERVES: 4

625 g (1¼ lb) lean minced beef
1 teaspoon finely grated fresh
   root ginger
2 teaspoons fennel seeds
1 teaspoon ground cinnamon
1 teaspoon turmeric
2 tablespoons mild curry powder
500 ml (17 fl oz) tomato passata
salt and pepper
low-fat yogurt, to drizzle
mint leaves, to garnish

To serve
Indian flatbread
salad

Small, spicy balls of minced beef cooked in a smooth sauce make a warming supper. Serve with Indian flatbreads and a fresh Indian salad or salsa. Wrap the koftas and salad in the bread for an informal meal.

Put the mince and ginger in a large mixing bowl. Roughly crush the fennel seeds in a mortar and pestle and add them to the meat mixture with the cinnamon. Season to taste with salt and pepper and use your hands to mix thoroughly. Form the mixture into small, walnut-sized balls and set aside.

Put the turmeric, curry powder and passata in a large, heavy-based saucepan and bring to the boil. Season, reduce the heat and carefully place the meatballs in the sauce. Cover and cook gently for 15–20 minutes, stirring and turning the meatballs around occasionally, until they are cooked through.

Remove from the heat, drizzle with yogurt and scatter with the mint leaves. Serve with chapattis or other flatbreads and salad.

light bites

If it's time to eat but you're not sure what you feel like, try one of the recipes in this chapter. Suitable for snacks, lunches or laid-back suppers, you're guaranteed to find something to tantalise your taste buds. There are lovely light salads such as *Chicken, Mangetout and Peach Salad* and quick snacks such as *Sardine Sorter*.

$\mathcal{R}$ose Gray's
sea bass baked in salt

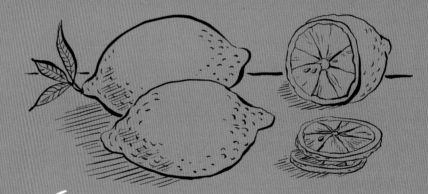

" I have selected this recipe as it's fresh and delicate with a delicious taste and texture. It's a healthy and simple dish that I enjoyed eating when I was ill, and it's also one of my favourite recipes to make and serve with *salsa verde* to share with friends. "

PREP: 25 MINUTES
COOKING TIME: ABOUT
25 MINUTES
SERVES: 4

1 lemon, sliced

50 g (2 oz) fennel stalks

2 kg (4 lb) whole sea bass, not
    scaled

3.5 kg (7 lb) coarse preserving
    salt

2 lemons, halved, to serve

Salsa verde

2 tablespoons parsley leaves,
    finely chopped

1 tablespoon mint leaves, finely
    chopped

1 tablespoon basil leaves, finely
    chopped

5 tablespoons extra virgin
    olive oil

1 garlic clove, chopped

1 tablespoon capers, chopped

3 anchovy fillets, chopped

1 tablespoon Dijon mustard

1 tablespoon red wine vinegar

pepper

Make the salsa. Put the herbs in a bowl and cover with the olive oil. Add the garlic, capers and anchovies to the herbs and mix. Stir in the mustard and vinegar, season to taste with pepper and add more olive oil to loosen the sauce if necessary.

Put the lemon slices and fennel stalks inside the cavity of the fish. Cover the bottom of a baking dish with half the salt and lay the bass on the salt. Cover the fish completely with the remaining salt in a layer about 1.5 cm (¾ inch) thick. Do not worry if the head and tail protrude. Sprinkle the surface of the salt with a little water.

Cook the fish in a preheated oven, 200°C (400°F), Gas Mark 6 for 25–30 minutes. Insert a skewer into the fish: if the tip of the skewer is warm, the fish is cooked.

Leave the fish to cool for 5 minutes, then crack open the salt crust and remove the salt. Make sure that no salt remains on the flesh of the fish. Carefully lift the fish from the dish, place it on a platter and remove and discard the skin. Serve at room temperature with the salsa.

panzanella

PREP: 15 MINUTES, PLUS
STANDING
COOKING TIME: 3–5 MINUTES
SERVES: 4

250 g (8 oz) ciabatta or country-
  style bread

100 ml (3½ fl oz) olive oil

500 g (1 lb) ripe tomatoes,
  skinned

½ small red onion, thinly sliced

handful of basil leaves, shredded

25 g (1 oz) anchovy fillets,
  drained and roughly chopped

2 tablespoons capers

1 garlic clove, crushed

2–3 tablespoons red wine vinegar

salt and pepper

Ripe tomatoes and slightly stale country bread can be put to good use in this rustic Italian salad, which is ideal for lunch, a light supper or an appetizing starter.

Tear the bread into small pieces. Scatter them on a baking sheet and drizzle with 1 tablespoon oil. Grill until lightly browned.

Roughly chop the tomatoes and tip them into a salad bowl with any juices. Add the onion, basil leaves, anchovies and capers. Scatter with the bread.

Whisk the remaining oil with the garlic, 2 tablespoons vinegar and salt and pepper to taste. (Add another tablespoon vinegar if you prefer a slightly tangier flavour.)

Drizzle the dressing over the salad and toss together lightly. Leave to stand for 20–30 minutes before serving.

shiitake mushroom
omelette

PREP: 5 MINUTES
COOKING TIME: ABOUT 5 MINUTES
SERVES: 2

2 teaspoons sesame oil

125 g (4 oz) shiitake mushrooms,
    sliced

3 tablespoons chopped chives,
    plus extra to garnish

1 teaspoon miso paste

5 eggs, lightly beaten

pepper

Even the most basic of dishes can be given a more exotic twist with a little imagination. If you can't get hold of shiitake mushrooms, chestnut mushrooms, finely sliced, will work just as well.

Heat the oil in a nonstick frying pan over a medium heat, add the mushrooms and chives and stir-fry for 2 minutes.

Dissolve the miso in 50 ml (2 fl oz) boiling water and add to the pan. Continue to fry until the liquid has evaporated.

Pour the eggs over the mushroom mixture and swirl around the pan to form a thin omelette. Cook for 1 minute.

Remove the pan from the heat and slide the omelette on to a plate. Roll up and sprinkle with pepper and a few extra chives.

red pepper soup
with croutons

PREP: 15 MINUTES
COOKING TIME: 45 MINUTES
SERVES: 6

4 tablespoons olive oil, plus extra
    for drizzling
2 red onions, sliced
5 red peppers, deseeded and
    roughly chopped
2 teaspoons caster sugar
2 garlic cloves, chopped
2 tablespoons chopped oregano,
    plus extra to garnish
900 ml (1½ pints) chicken or
    vegetable stock
400 g (13 oz) can chopped
    tomatoes
2 tablespoons sun-dried tomato
    paste
6 thin slices of baguette
salt and pepper

For best results use 'pointed' red peppers, which are sweet and have a fuller flavour than the round ones. Gently sautéing the peppers and onion in the oil will intensify the flavour of the soup.

Heat 4 tablespoons oil in a large saucepan. Add the onions and red peppers and cook gently, stirring frequently, for 10 minutes. Add the sugar, garlic and oregano and fry for a further 5–10 minutes or until the peppers are soft.

Add the stock, tomatoes, tomato paste and a little salt and pepper and bring to the boil. Reduce the heat and simmer gently for 20 minutes.

Use a stick blender to blend the soup until pulpy. Alternatively, blend the soup in batches in a food processor.

Toast the bread on both sides for 2–3 minutes.

Reheat the soup and ladle it into warm individual bowls. Add a piece of toast to each one, drizzle with a little oil and serve scattered with chopped oregano.

> ❝ I have worked on the helpline at Breast Cancer Care for eight years now, and at the end of a shift we often share our supper recipes. The capacity to enjoy good food is one of the great pleasures in life and I am thankful for it. ❞
>
> **Helen Brahmbhatt, Breast Cancer Care helpline worker, diagnosed 1997**

chicken soup ✳

PREP: 20 MINUTES
COOKING TIME: 50 MINUTES
SERVES: 4

25 g (1 oz) butter
1 onion, chopped
1 celery stick, chopped
1 carrot, chopped
1 teaspoon ground cinnamon
2 x 410 g (13½ oz) cans
    chickpeas, rinsed and drained
1 litre (1¾ pints) chicken stock
1 chicken breast
125 g (4 oz) chorizo sausage,
    chopped
salt and pepper
snipped chives, to garnish

Heat half the butter in a large, heavy-based pan and gently fry the onion, celery and carrot until they are soft. Add the cinnamon and stir to mix.

Add the chickpeas and one-third of the stock to the pan. When it is hot, transfer to a food processor or use a stick blender to make a smooth mixture. If necessary, return the mixture to the pan and cook for a little longer. Add the remaining stock to the pan and cook for a further 30 minutes.

Meanwhile, heat the remaining butter in a separate frying pan and gently fry the chicken until it is cooked through. Cut the chicken into small pieces and add them to the soup with the chorizo. Season to taste with salt and pepper and cook for a further 10 minutes.

Sprinkle with chives and serve with crusty wholemeal bread.

watermelon and
feta salad

PREP: 10 MINUTES
COOKING TIME: 2 MINUTES
SERVES: 4

1 tablespoon black sesame
seeds
500 g (1 lb) watermelon, peeled,
deseeded and diced
175 g (6 oz) feta cheese, diced
250 g (8 oz) rocket leaves
handful of mint, parsley and fresh
coriander sprigs
6 tablespoons extra virgin olive
oil
1 tablespoon orange flower water
1½ tablespoons lemon juice
1 teaspoon pomegranate syrup
(optional)
½ teaspoon sugar
salt and pepper
toasted pitta bread, to serve

Dry-fry the sesame seeds for a few minutes until aromatic, then set aside. Arrange the watermelon and feta on a large plate with the rocket and herbs.

Whisk together the oil, orange flower water, lemon juice, pomegranate syrup (if used) and sugar, then season to taste with salt and pepper. Drizzle the dressing over the salad, scatter over the sesame seeds and serve with toasted pitta bread.

pork kofte
kebabs

PREP: 10 MINUTES, PLUS CHILLING
COOKING TIME: 15–20 MINUTES
SERVES: 4

250 g (8 oz) minced lean pork
1 large onion, quartered
1 garlic clove, halved
1 chilli, cored and deseeded
2 teaspoons tomato purée
15 g (½ oz) fresh coriander
15 g (½ oz) parsley
salt and pepper
vegetable oil, for greasing

This recipe can be used to make homemade burgers, and you can vary the herbs and spices as well as the meat: chicken, beef and lamb work well.

Put all the ingredients in a food processor or blender and process to make a smooth paste.

Divide the meat mixture into four pieces and form each portion around a skewer. Cover the kebabs and refrigerate until they are needed.

Brush a foil-lined grill pan with oil and cook the kebabs under a preheated moderately hot grill for 15–20 minutes, turning them several times until they have browned on the outside and are thoroughly cooked through. Serve immediately.

spicy lentil and
haloumi salad

PREP: 15 MINUTES
COOKING TIME: 25 MINUTES
SERVES: 4

225 g (7½ oz) Puy lentils

1 tablespoon vegetable bouillon powder

3 bay leaves

1 onion, halved

225 g (7½ oz) haloumi cheese

100 ml (3½ fl oz) olive oil

2 teaspoons coriander seeds

2 teaspoons cumin seeds

1 bunch of spring onions, thinly sliced

finely grated rind of 1 lemon, plus 4 tablespoons juice

2 tablespoons clear honey

2 celery sticks, very thinly sliced

4 tablespoons chopped fresh coriander

pepper

Salty haloumi cheese and a sweet and tangy dressed lentil salad make a delicious balance of flavours in this nourishing dish. It can be served warm, freshly prepared, but is also good chilled.

Rinse the lentils and put them in a saucepan with the bouillon powder, bay leaves and onion and cover with plenty of cold water. Bring to the boil, reduce the heat and simmer gently for 20 minutes until the lentils are tender. Drain, discarding the onion but leaving the bay leaves, and tip the lentils into a bowl.

Pat the haloumi between several sheets of kitchen paper to remove the moisture, then cut it into small chunks. Heat 1 tablespoon oil in a frying pan and fry the cheese on all sides until the pieces are beginning to brown.

Crush the seeds using a pestle and mortar. Tip them into a small saucepan and add the remaining oil and the spring onions. Heat gently for 30 seconds for the flavours to infuse together. Remove the pan from the heat and add the lemon rind and juice and honey. Season with plenty of pepper.

Pour the dressing over the lentils and add the celery, coriander and haloumi. Toss the ingredients together and serve warm or cold.

waldorf salad

PREP: 15 MINUTES
NO COOK
SERVES: 4

4 unpeeled dessert apples, cored
and cut into cubes

1 celery heart, cut into cubes

small bunch of grapes, halved
and deseeded

50 g (2 oz) walnuts or pecan nuts,
coarsely chopped

3 tablespoons mayonnaise

This classic American salad, which was invented at the Waldorf-Astoria Hotel in New York in the 1890s, is an all-time favourite.

Mix the apples, celery, grapes and nuts with the mayonnaise, keeping some of the nuts as a topping.

Spoon the salad into bowls and top with the rest of the nuts. Serve immediately.

farfalle
with tuna sauce

PREP: 10 MINUTES, PLUS
STANDING
COOKING TIME: 3–10 MINUTES
SERVES: 4

125 g (4 oz) can tuna in olive oil,
    drained
2 tablespoons extra virgin olive
    oil, plus extra to serve
    (optional)
4 tomatoes, roughly chopped
50 g (2 oz) pitted black olives,
    roughly chopped
grated rind of 1 lemon
2 garlic cloves, crushed
2 tablespoons roughly chopped
    flat leaf parsley
350 g (11½ oz) dried farfalle
salt

Good-quality Italian, Spanish and Portuguese canned tuna in olive oil are truly delicious. Try it in this raw pasta sauce – it is ideal for a light supper in summer. To serve this dish as a pasta salad, refresh the cooked pasta in cold running water before adding the remaining ingredients.

Put the tuna in a large serving bowl. Break it up with a fork, then stir in the remaining ingredients, except for the pasta. Season to taste with salt, cover and leave to stand for the flavours to infuse for at least 30 minutes.

Meanwhile, cook the pasta in a large saucepan of lightly salted boiling water, allowing 3 minutes for fresh pasta and 8–10 minutes for dried or according to packet instructions. Drain thoroughly and toss into the sauce.

Serve immediately with a drizzle of extra virgin olive oil, if liked.

> *Having been through the rigours of breast cancer, I learned to take a new look at the food I was eating. I realized that fish didn't feature very much in my diet and sardines seemed to tick all the right boxes.*
> **Paula Snow, diagnosed 2003**

sardine sorter ✿

PREP: 5 MINUTES
NO COOK
SERVES: 3–4

2 x 125 g (4 oz) cans sardines
   in oil
2 tablespoons balsamic vinegar
1 tablespoon Japanese soy
   sauce
handful fresh coriander, chopped
2–3 spring onions, chopped
1 medium-strength red chilli,
   deseeded and chopped
   (optional)

To serve
toast
watercress and rocket salad
French dressing

If you don't want to serve these tasty sardines on toast, wrap a tablespoon of the sardine mix in a large lettuce leaf and tie into a parcel with a long slice of spring onion – a perfect late supper after that big lunch.

Drain a little oil from the sardines and put them in a bowl. Mash them together with a fork and beat in the balsamic vinegar, soy sauce and coriander. Add the spring onions and chilli (if used).

Alternatively, put the sardines, vinegar and soy sauce in a food processor and blend until smooth and pale in colour, then whiz in the coriander, chilli (if used) and spring onions until combined.

Serve the mix on hot toast with a watercress and rocket salad with French dressing.

chicken, mangetout and
peach salad

PREP: 15 MINUTES
COOKING TIME: ABOUT
10 MINUTES
SERVES: 4

200 g (7 oz) dried pasta shapes,
    such as rigatoni, lumaconi or
    trompretti
125 g (4 oz) mangetout, sliced
    diagonally
2 large, juicy peaches, skinned,
    halved and stoned
200 g (7 oz) lean, cooked chicken,
    roughly sliced
½ bunch of spring onions, sliced
    diagonally
15 g (½ oz) fresh coriander leaves,
    chopped
salt and pepper

Dressing
3 tablespoons clear honey
3 tablespoons lemon juice
4 tablespoons mild olive oil
1 tablespoon soy sauce
2 teaspoons Thai fish sauce

This salad is a delicious concoction of complementary colours and flavours, from the sweet and juicy peaches to the saltiness of the dressing.

Bring a large saucepan of lightly salted water to the boil, add the pasta and cook for 8–10 minutes or according to packet instructions until just tender. Add the mangetout and cook for a further 1 minute. Drain and rinse under cold running water. Drain thoroughly and turn into a large bowl.

Cut the peach flesh into slices and add them to the bowl with the chicken, spring onions and coriander.

Make the dressing by whisking together the honey, lemon juice, olive oil, soy sauce and Thai fish sauce.

Just before serving, pour the dressing over the salad, season with pepper and toss the ingredients together well.

avocado, crab and
coriander salad

PREP: 10 MINUTES
NO COOK
SERVES: 4

1 head curly endive

175 g (6 oz) lamb's lettuce or
   baby spinach leaves

1 large, ripe avocado, sliced

300 g (10 oz) crab meat

1 large mango, about 300 g
   (10 oz), cubed

175 g (6 oz) cherry tomatoes,
   halved

freshly grated nutmeg

salt and pepper

Dressing

5 tablespoons olive oil

1 tablespoon lime juice

3 tablespoons chopped fresh
   coriander

1 small red chilli, deseeded and
   finely chopped (optional)

This is a very satisfying salad and an excellent choice for lunch. If you are feeling extravagant, buy four extra crab claws and add them to the finished dish.

Make the dressing. Put all the ingredients in a jar and shake until well combined or whiz them briefly in a blender.

Arrange the endive and lamb's lettuce on 4 serving plates and scatter the avocado, crab meat, mango and tomatoes over each portion.

Season to taste with salt, pepper and nutmeg. Drizzle over the dressing and serve.

lemon and couscous stuffed
tomatoes

PREP: 10 MINUTES, PLUS
STANDING
NO COOK
MAKES: 20

10 tomatoes, each about 3.5 cm
   (1½ inches) in diameter
50 g (2 oz) couscous
2 tablespoons olive oil
1 preserved lemon
3 tablespoons finely chopped
   mint
salt and pepper
tiny mint leaves, to garnish
   (optional)

Preserved lemons are used in all kinds of Moroccan dishes. They provide an almost creamy citrus flavour and go well with chicken, lamb and vegetables.

Cut the tomatoes in half and, using a small spoon, scoop out and discard the seeds. Put the tomato shells, cut side down, on a piece of kitchen paper and set aside.

Put the couscous in a small heatproof bowl, stir in the oil and pour over boiling water just to cover. Cover with clingfilm and leave to stand for 8–10 minutes to absorb the water.

Dice the preserved lemon finely, discarding any seeds. Fluff up the couscous with a fork, stir in the lemon and mint and season well with salt and pepper.

Put the tomato halves on a serving platter. Using a small teaspoon, spoon some of the couscous mixture into each tomato shell, garnish with mint leaves (if used) and serve at room temperature.

> " It's almost as if a door has closed in my mind on the traumatic time of cancer and chemo. Once I was on the mend this was – and is – one of my favourite dinner party recipes. Welcoming family and friends and sharing time with them is a very special kind of therapy! "
>
> **Susan Woodcock**, touched by breast cancer

baked cod ✿

PREP: 15 MINUTES
COOKING TIME: 20 MINUTES
SERVES: 6

6 pieces of cod (tails if possible),
    about 200 g (7 oz) each, skin
    removed
olive oil, for greasing and dipping

Tapenade
25 g (1 oz) basil
185 g (6¼ oz) pitted olives
275 g (9 oz) sun-dried tomatoes
    in oil
2 garlic cloves, chopped
3 tablespoons capers, drained
    and dried
25g (1 oz) fresh basil, chopped
black pepper

Make the tapenade, reserving 6 whole basil leaves, 6 whole olives and the oil from the tomatoes. Put the basil, olives, drained tomatoes, garlic and capers and 3 tablespoons oil from the tomatoes in a food processor and blend to make a rough paste.

Clean the fish, tuck the sides or tail under to form each into a rounded shape and place them on a lightly oiled baking sheet. Divide the tapenade into 6 portions and use your hands to make each into a ball. Press these on the fish and flatten slightly. Garnish each with a reserved basil leaf dipped in olive oil and topped with a whole olive.

Bake the fish on the top shelf of a preheated oven, 200°C (400°F), Gas Mark 6, for 20-25 minutes.

Reserve the juices from the cooked fish and serve as a sauce together with creamy layer potatoes and green beans.

*H*ugh Johnson's
hot ham mousse

' This is comfort food, using leftovers –
two recommendations already. And it is
delicious, especially with sauté potatoes and
spinach. A good red, such as Chianti, does no
harm either. I dedicate it to our friends who
have had breast cancer. '

PREP: 10 MINUTES
COOKING TIME: ABOUT
35 MINUTES
SERVES: 4–6

300 g (10 oz) cooked ham
1 teaspoon French mustard
2 eggs
250 ml (8 fl oz) milk
pepper

Process the cooked ham in a blender until it is in small pieces (as if minced). Season with pepper and transfer to a bowl.

Put the mustard, eggs and milk into a blender and process for a few seconds. Add to the ham and mix together.

Transfer the mixture to a lightly greased soufflé dish and bake in a preheated oven, 220°C (425°F), Gas Mark 7, for about 35–40 minutes. The mousse should still be runny in the middle.

fresh spring rolls

PREP: 20 MINUTES, PLUS SOAKING
NO COOK
MAKES: 8 ROLLS; SERVES 4 AS A
STARTER

6 dried Chinese mushrooms

50 g (2 oz) thin rice noodles

8 round dried rice paper sheets,
    22 cm (8½ inches) across

250 g (8 oz) fresh bean sprouts

1 small cucumber, cut into strips

2 tablespoons roughly torn mint
    leaves

2 tablespoons roughly torn fresh
    coriander leaves

1 carrot, grated

2 tablespoons roasted unsalted
    peanuts, coarsely chopped

Spring rolls are a firm favourite at Chinese restaurants and takeaways. This version is adapted from a Vietnamese recipe and uses soft rice paper sheets stuffed with fresh herbs and crunchy vegetables.

Put the dried mushrooms in a heatproof bowl, cover them with boiling water and put a plate on top to keep in the steam. Set aside for 20–30 minutes or until soft. Drain the mushrooms, discard the stalks and squeeze the water from the caps, then shred them finely.

Place the rice noodles in a bowl, pour over some boiling water and leave to stand, covered, for about 10 minutes. Drain the noodles, rinse with cold water and set aside.

Soak the sheets of rice paper in a bowl of warm water, one at a time, for 30–60 seconds until softened, then transfer them to a clean, dry tea towel.

Prepare the spring rolls. Put a little of all the filling ingredients on each rice paper sheet, roll up the bottom half of the rice paper, fold in the sides and roll over to enclose the filling.

gado gado

PREP: 20 MINUTES
COOKING TIME: ABOUT
18 MINUTES
SERVES: 6–8

2 carrots, peeled and cut into
thick 5 cm (2 inch) long fingers
100 g (3½ oz) long green beans,
cut into 5 cm (2 inch) lengths
2 large potatoes, peeled and cut
into thick 5 cm (2 inch) long
fingers
1 cucumber, cut into thick, 5 cm
(2 inch) long fingers
200 g (7 oz) ready-prepared fried
bean curd, cut into bite-sized
cubes
salt

Spicy dipping sauce
2 tablespoons kecap manis
(sweet soy sauce)
4 tablespoons dark soy sauce
1 teaspoon sambal oelek (hot
chilli paste)

Peanut dipping sauce
4 tablespoons smooth peanut
butter
2 tablespoons sweet chilli sauce
3 tablespoons light soy sauce

This typical Indonesian dish is often served garnished with hard-boiled egg and potatoes, making it a filling main meal.

Bring a large saucepan of lightly salted water to the boil, add the carrots and long beans and blanch for 2–3 minutes. Drain and refresh in cold water. Cook the potatoes in lightly salted, boiling water for about 15 minutes or until just tender, then drain and set aside. Arrange all the vegetables on a serving platter with the bean curd.

Make the spicy dipping sauce by combining all the ingredients in a small bowl.

Make the peanut dipping sauce by mixing the peanut butter with the chilli and soy sauces. Pour in 50 ml (2 fl oz) boiling water, stir to mix well and transfer to a small bowl.

Serve the vegetables with the two dipping sauces.

Rose Elliot's
honeydew melon, strawberry and mint compote

" When you're feeling under the weather and not fancying much, this might hit the spot. It's so refreshing and uplifting, and it's wonderful to have a bowl of it in the refrigerator so you can help yourself as and when you feel like it. Honeydew melons are at their sweetest and most melting in mid- to late summer; at other times, choose the most luscious type available. "

PREP: 15 MINUTES, PLUS
STANDING
NO COOK
SERVES: 4

20 g (¾ oz) mint, leaves only

75 g (3 oz) caster sugar or clear
    honey

1 ripe honeydew melon (or other
    sweet, ripe melon)

500 g (1 lb) strawberries, hulled
    and sliced

Put the mint leaves in a large bowl and crush them lightly with the end of
a rolling pin or a wooden spoon. Add the sugar or honey and crush the
leaves again by pressing them against the side of the bowl with a
wooden spoon. Set aside.

Halve the melon and scoop out and discard the seeds. Scoop out the
flesh with a melon-baller or use a sharp knife to cut it away from the skin
and into bite-sized pieces.

Put the melon pieces in a bowl with the mint and add the strawberries.
Stir, cover and leave for 1–4 hours for the flavours to blend. The fruit
compote will produce its own liquid, and it is deliciously refreshing served
cold but not icy.

quick and easy

Whilst it's always wonderful to sit down to a home-cooked meal you might not have the time or inclination to spend hours in the kitchen. All the recipes in this chapter, from *Traditional Steak and Vegetables* to *Cheat's Cheesecake*, can be prepared in minutes or left to cook while you get on with other things.

pan-fried
chicken thighs
with fresh pesto

PREP: 10 MINUTES
COOKING TIME: 25 MINUTES
SERVES: 4

1 tablespoon olive oil
8 chicken thighs
basil leaves, to garnish

Pesto
6 tablespoons olive oil
50 g (2 oz) pine nuts, toasted
50 g (2 oz) freshly grated
   Parmesan cheese
50 g (2 oz) basil leaves
15 g (½ oz) parsley
2 garlic cloves, chopped
salt and pepper

This quick, inexpensive dish is great served with fresh vegetables or a spinach salad. If you want to make it even easier, buy a jar of good-quality pesto – a couple of tablespoons per portion will do the job perfectly.

Heat the oil in a nonstick frying pan over a medium heat. Add the chicken thighs and cook gently, turning frequently, for about 20 minutes or until the chicken is cooked through.

Meanwhile, make the pesto by placing all the ingredients in a blender or food processor and whizzing until smooth and well combined.

Remove the chicken from the pan and keep hot. Reduce the heat and add the pesto to the pan. Heat through for 2–3 minutes.

Pour the warmed pesto over the chicken thighs, garnish with basil and serve with steamed vegetables.

' I had not eaten red meat for years, despite wanting to. On getting a diagnosis of cancer I gave myself permission to eat whatever I wanted. I ate organic steak a few times before surgery and I felt as if I was building up my strength as well as really enjoying myself. '

Gail Simon, diagnosed 2006

traditional
steak ✶
and vegetables

PREP: 5 MINUTES
COOKING TIME: 15 MINUTES
SERVES: 2

1 teaspoon black peppercorns
2 x 175–250 g (6–8 oz) organic
   sirloin steaks
2 carrots
2 courgettes
salt

Grind the peppercorns using a pestle and mortar. Brush the steaks with the oil and season with the crushed pepercorns and a little salt. Set aside.

Cut the carrots and courgettes into batons. Steam the carrots for 5 minutes then add the courgettes and cook for a further 8–10 minutes until just tender.

Meanwhile, the steaks in a preheated griddle pan or under a preheated medium grill for 2–4 minutes on each side, adjusting the timing according to your preference for well-done or rare meat. Serve with the vegetables.

pumpkin soup

with harissa

PREP: 25 MINUTES
COOKING TIME: 35 MINUTES
SERVES: 6

1 kg (2 lb) pumpkin

4 tablespoons olive oil

2 onions, chopped

2 garlic cloves, crushed

1 litre (1¾ pints) vegetable stock

100 ml (3½ fl oz) double cream

salt and pepper

1 quantity Hot Harissa Sauce (see
    page 85), to serve

chopped fresh coriander, to
    garnish

This smooth and creamy soup is zipped up with harissa sauce, which is stirred in at the table to add a spicy edge. Serve the extra sauce in a bowl for those who like a hotter flavour.

Scoop out the seeds and cut away the skin from the pumpkin. Chop the flesh into chunks.

Heat the oil in a large, heavy-based saucepan and gently fry the onions for 5 minutes. Add the garlic and fry for a further 1 minute. Add the pumpkin and stock and bring to the boil. Reduce the heat, cover with a lid and cook gently for 20–25 minutes or until the pumpkin is soft and mushy.

Use a stick blender to blend the soup until pulpy. Alternatively, whiz it in batches in a food processor. Return the soup to the saucepan, stir in half the cream and season to taste with salt and pepper. Reheat gently.

Ladle the soup into warm individual soup bowls and spoon a little of the harissa sauce over each. Drizzle with the remaining cream and serve scattered with coriander.

hot harissa
sauce

PREP: 10 MINUTES, PLUS CHILLING
COOKING TIME: 5 MINUTES
SERVES: 4–6

1 tablespoon coriander seeds

1 teaspoon caraway seeds

3 tablespoons light olive oil

1 red pepper, deseeded and
    roughly chopped

1 small red onion, roughly
    chopped

1 red chilli, deseeded and
    chopped

3 garlic cloves, chopped

4 tablespoons coriander leaves,
    torn into pieces

½ teaspoon celery salt

150 ml (5 oz) tomato passata

This is a quick and easy sauce with plenty of flavour. Use the entire mixture to stir into sautéed vegetables and beans or as a wonderful couscous topping. Alternatively, use smaller quantities to zip up soups and stews.

Use a pestle and mortar to grind the coriander and caraway seeds until lightly crushed. Alternatively, use a small bowl and the end of a rolling pin.

Tip the seeds into a small frying pan and add the oil, red pepper and onion. Cook gently for 5 minutes or until the vegetables are soft.

Transfer the mixture to a food processor or blender and add the chilli, garlic, coriander, celery salt and passata.

Blend the soup until smooth, scraping the mixture down from the sides of the bowl if necessary. Transfer it to a serving bowl, cover with clingfilm and chill until ready to serve.

greek wrap

PREP: 5 MINUTES
NO COOK
SERVES: 2

75 g (3 oz) feta cheese
2 tortillas
2 tomatoes, sliced
½ red onion, finely sliced
10 black olives, pitted and halved
handful of baby spinach leaves
olive oil, to drizzle

Really simple and quick to make, this is so delightfully fresh-tasting that it is perfect for lunch on a warm summer's day.

Crumble the feta over the tortillas. Add the tomatoes, onion, olives and spinach leaves, then drizzle with olive oil.

Wrap the tortillas round the filling and eat immediately.

*L*orraine Kelly's
thai green curry paste

PREP: 15 MINUTES
NO COOK
SERVES: 4–6

15 green chillies, chopped

4 spring onions or 1 large onion, chopped

3 garlic cloves, roughly chopped

1 tablespoon olive oil

1 tablespoon chopped galangal or ginger

2 tablespoons Thai fish sauce

1 tablespoon caster sugar

1 teaspoon blachan (shrimp paste) or 2 teaspoons dried shrimps

3 lemon grass stalks, crushed

1 teaspoon ground coriander

4 tablespoons or 1 bunch of fresh coriander leaves, chopped

juice and grated rind of 2 limes

3 fresh kaffir lime leaves (optional)

The green of this paste comes from the fresh coriander leaves. Like all plant materials, the natural chlorophyll (green colour) oxidizes in air, fading rapidly on picking and cooking. Although this paste will keep for up to a week in the refrigerator, it should be used within two days for maximum impact, colour and flavour. It is best used for the clear, hot, sour-sweet curries much beloved of the Thais.

Put all the ingredients in a blender or food processor and liquidize or process to a smooth paste.

Add the paste to any ingredients you like, such as lightly fried strips of chicken breast or beef with green and red peppers, onions and baby sweetcorn.

Serve with Thai fragrant rice.

super club

with grainy mustard

PREP: 10 MINUTES
COOKING TIME: 3–4 MINUTES
SERVES: 2

50 ml (2 fl oz) mayonnaise, plus
extra to serve

2 tablespoons wholegrain
mustard, plus extra to serve

4 slices of multigrain bread

2 slices of honey-roast ham

75 g (3 oz) deli-style turkey, in
wafer-thin slices

75 g (3 oz) strong Cheddar
cheese, finely sliced

1 large beefsteak tomato, sliced

½ small red onion, finely sliced

6 rashers of cooked, smoked
bacon

6 cornichons or gherkins, finely
sliced (optional)

2 tablespoons chopped chives

Combine the mayonnaise and mustard in a small bowl and spread the mixture over one side of each slice of bread.

Arrange the ham slices on 2 slices of bread, followed by the sliced turkey. Top with the Cheddar and tomato and scatter over the onion. Next, top with the bacon and cornichon slices (if used), then sprinkle the chives over the filling and cover with the remaining slices of bread.

Toast in a sandwich grill for 3–4 minutes, or according to the manufacturer's instructions, until the filling is hot and melting and the bread is golden. Serve immediately with extra mayonnaise and mustard.

Denise Welch's
tuna pasta

PREP: 5 MINUTES
COOKING TIME: ABOUT
15 MINUTES
SERVES: 2

200 g (7 oz) pasta
25 g (1 oz) butter
200 g (7 oz) can tuna in oil,
    drained and flaked
125 g (4 oz) Cheddar cheese,
    grated
salt and pepper

Cook the pasta in lightly salted boiling water according to the directions on the packet. Drain.

Add the butter to the saucepan and heat gently to melt. Roughly flake the tuna and add to the pan with the oil from the can.

Return the drained pasta to the saucepan with the cheese and mix well over a gentle heat. Season with salt and pepper and serve immediately.

Ainsley Harriott's

crispy corned beef and beet hash

' Beef hash is a great breakfast or brunch treat. It's outstanding for tastiness and economy and is popular in the US. The addition of beetroot makes this crunchy version turn a wicked purple-red colour. You could leave the beet out, but don't knock it till you've tried it. '

PREP: 10 MINUTES
COOKING TIME: 25 MINUTES
SERVES: 4

500 g (1 lb) floury potatoes
3 tablespoons olive oil
2 onions, sliced
350 g (11½ oz) can corned beef,
   diced
150 g (5 oz) cooked beetroot,
   diced
1 tablespoon chopped parsley
salt and pepper

Peel the potatoes and cut them into large dice. Cook them in lightly salted, boiling water for about 10 minutes or until they are just tender. Drain in a colander.

Meanwhile, heat the oil in a large frying pan and cook the onions over a medium heat until they are just beginning to brown at the edges.

Add the potatoes to the frying pan and cook for 2 minutes. Add the corned beef and beetroot, mix well and cook for 3–4 minutes without turning to allow the bottom of the mixture to become crispy.

Cook for a further 10 minutes, stirring as little as possible, so that the potatoes, corned beef and beet cook through and the mixture has plenty of crispy bits throughout.

Season to taste with salt and pepper, scatter with parsley and serve with sunnyside-up fried eggs.

salmon

roasted with fennel, vine tomatoes and red onions

PREP: 10 MINUTES
COOKING TIME: 22–25 MINUTES
SERVES: 4

4 salmon fillets, 175–250 g
   (6–8 oz) each
4 tablespoons lemon juice
4 tablespoons olive oil
1 tablespoon balsamic vinegar
1 tablespoon honey
4 garlic cloves, finely chopped
2 red onions, quartered
2 fennel bulbs, quartered
16–20 cherry vine tomatoes
salt and pepper
rice or couscous, to serve

Season the salmon fillets generously with salt and pepper and pour the lemon juice over them. Set aside.

Combine the olive oil, balsamic vinegar, honey and garlic in a small bowl and season with salt and pepper. Put the onions, fennel and tomatoes in a bowl and pour over the oil mixture. Toss to coat thoroughly, then spread on a baking sheet. Place in a preheated oven, 220°C (425°F), Gas Mark 7, and roast for 10 minutes. Add the salmon fillets to the baking sheet and roast for a further 12–15 minutes.

Remove the salmon from the oven when it is cooked through and serve with the roasted vegetables accompanied with rice or couscous.

swordfish

with lemon, olives and capers

PREP: 15 MINUTES, PLUS
MARINATING
COOKING TIME: 4–6 MINUTES
SERVES: 4

1 tablespoon olive oil

2 tablespoons lemon juice

½ red chilli, deseeded and
    chopped

4 swordfish steaks, about 175 g
    (6 oz) each

rind of 1 lemon, roughly chopped

1 garlic clove, roughly chopped

2½ tablespoons capers, soaked,
    drained and roughly chopped

10 pitted black olives, roughly
    chopped

1 tablespoon roughly chopped
    mint

extra virgin olive oil, for drizzling
    (optional)

salt

Swordfish has a meaty texture that benefits from quick searing so that the flesh retains its juiciness. This flavoursome topping is a favourite in Sicily and is just as delicious scattered over griddled tuna, chicken breast or steak.

Mix together the olive oil, lemon juice and chilli and pour into a large, non-metallic dish. Add the swordfish steaks and turn them in the marinade so that they are coated on both sides. Cover and leave to marinate for 15 minutes.

Meanwhile, make the topping by combining the lemon rind, garlic, capers, olives and mint.

Heat a ridged cast-iron griddle pan over a high heat. Lightly season the steaks with salt, add them to the pan and cook for 2–3 minutes on each side so that they are just cooked through.

Serve the swordfish with a scattering of the topping and a drizzle of extra virgin olive oil, if liked.

eggs florentine

PREP: 15 MINUTES
COOKING TIME: 20–22 MINUTES
SERVES: 6

40 g (1½ oz) butter

1 kg (2 lb) fresh spinach, washed

2 large tomatoes, skinned and
   diced

freshly grated nutmeg

6 large eggs

150 ml (¼ pint) crème fraîche

50 ml (2 fl oz) double cream

40 g (1½ oz) Cheddar cheese,
   grated

40 g (1½ oz) Parmesan cheese,
   grated

salt and pepper

Melt half the butter in a large, heavy-based saucepan. Add the fresh spinach with just the water that clings to the rinsed leaves. Cover tightly and sweat until the leaves have wilted, the spinach is tender and any liquid has evaporated. Transfer to a large sieve or colander and squeeze out any liquid that remains. Return the spinach to the pan, add the tomatoes and season with nutmeg, salt and pepper.

Grease 6 gratin dishes, each holding 175 ml (6 fl oz), with the remaining butter. Divide the spinach among the dishes, making a well in the centre of each for an egg and leaving a 1 cm (½ inch) space between the spinach and the rim of the dish.

Break an egg into the centre of each dish and dust with salt and pepper. Mix together the crème fraîche and cream. Spoon evenly over the eggs and sprinkle with the Cheddar and Parmesan.

Set the gratin dishes on a heavy baking sheet and bake in a preheated oven, 220°C (425°F), Gas Mark 7, for 10–12 minutes or until the whites are set but the yolks are still runny.

Remove the dishes from the oven and place under a preheated hot grill until the topping is bubbling and the cheese is golden-brown. Serve immediately.

> **'** I love to make this recipe – it's so simple and easy to make. **'**
> **Catriona Edwards**, touched by breast cancer

cod ❋
with mozzarella
and cherry tomatoes

PREP: 5 MINUTES
COOKING TIME: 20–25 MINUTES
SERVES: 1

olive oil, to drizzle
1 cod loin, about 200-225 g
    (7–7½ oz)
75 g (3 oz) mozzarella cheese,
    preferably buffalo
handful of cherry tomatoes, about
    75 g (3 oz)
chilli flakes (optional)
salt and pepper

Drizzle a little olive oil in a small ovenproof dish or over a baking sheet and put the cod on top.

Tear the mozzarella into small pieces and scatter it over the cod. Cut the tomatoes in half (you can leave some whole if you wish) and scatter them over and around the cod. Season to taste with salt and pepper and scatter over the chilli flakes (if used). Drizzle with a little more olive oil.

Cook the cod in a preheated oven, 180°C (350°F), Gas Mark 4, for about 15 minutes or until the fish starts to flake when pierced with a knife.

mozzarella and
tomato tartlets

PREP: 15 MINUTES
COOKING TIME: ABOUT
20 MINUTES
SERVES: 6

250 g (8 oz) puff pastry, thawed if
frozen

beaten egg or milk, to glaze

6 tablespoons sun-dried tomato
paste

3 plum tomatoes, deseeded and
roughly chopped

125 g (4 oz) mozzarella cheese,
roughly diced

8 black olives, pitted and roughly
chopped

1 garlic clove, finely chopped

2 tablespoons roughly chopped
oregano

1 tablespoon pine nuts

olive oil, to drizzle

salt and pepper

mixed salad leaves, to serve

These tartlets take next to no time to prepare but will make a delicious and filling lunch when served with a fresh, crisp salad.

Roll out the pastry on a lightly floured board to 3 mm (⅛ inch) thick. Use a round cutter to stamp out 6 circles, each 12 cm (5 inch) across, and put them on a prepared baking sheet. Use a sharp knife to make a shallow mark 1 cm (½ inch) in from the edge of each round to form a rim; do not cut right through the pastry. Brush the rims with beaten egg or milk.

Spread 1 tablespoon of tomato paste over each pastry circle. Mix together the tomatoes, mozzarella, olives, garlic, oregano and pine nuts in a small bowl and season to taste with salt and pepper.

Divide this mixture among the pastry circles and drizzle a little olive oil over the tartlets.

Bake the tartlets in a preheated oven, 200°C (400°F), Gas Mark 6, for 20 minutes or until the pastry has risen and is golden. Serve at once with mixed salad leaves.

fennel, orange and
olive salad

PREP: 15 MINUTES
NO COOK
SERVES: 2–4

1 large fennel bulb, about 325 g
  (11 oz), thinly sliced

8–10 black olives, pitted

1 tablespoon extra virgin olive oil

2 tablespoons lemon juice

2 oranges

salt and pepper

There is no more refreshing salad on a baking hot summer's day than this Sicilian combination. Serve it as a light lunch or as part of an antipasto selection.

Toss the fennel with the olives, oil and lemon juice in a large bowl. Season to taste with salt and pepper.

Working over a bowl to catch the juice and using a serrated knife, cut away the skin and pith of the oranges and slice the flesh thinly into rounds. Add the orange slices, along with any juice, to the fennel salad and toss gently to combine.

pan-seared beef

with garlic and chilli sauce

PREP: 20 MINUTES
COOKING TIME: 3–4 MINUTES
SERVES: 2

400 g (13 oz) sirloin beef, cut into
   1 cm (½ inch) thick slices
1 teaspoon sesame oil

Garlic and chilli dipping sauce
2 garlic cloves, crushed
1 tablespoon shoyu or tamari
   sauce
1 teaspoon light muscovado
   sugar
2 red chillies, deseeded and finely
   chopped
1 tablespoon lime juice

This recipe is an adaptation of the Thai dish known as 'shaking' beef, which gets its name from the sound of the pan being shaken as the beef is cooked. It goes well with boiled rice and stir-fried vegetables.

Beat the beef on both sides with a meat mallet to make it slightly thinner. Brush the beef with the sesame oil and set aside.

Meanwhile, make the dipping sauce by mixing together all the ingredients in a small bowl and set aside.

Put the beef slices on a preheated very hot griddle pan. For medium beef, cook for about 1½ minutes on each side until browned. Remove from the pan and let the beef rest for about 1 minute, then slice thinly into 1 cm (½ inch) strips.

Serve the beef with the dipping sauce.

fragrant aubergine
stir-fry

PREP: 15 MINUTES
COOKING TIME: 7 MINUTES
SERVES: 2

vegetable oil, for deep-frying

250 g (8 oz) aubergines, peeled and cut into chip-sized strips

2 spring onions, finely chopped

1 slice fresh root ginger, peeled and finely chopped

1 garlic clove, finely chopped

1 tablespoon soy sauce

2 teaspoons sweet chilli sauce

2 tablespoons cornflour

The crispiness of the aubergine chips and the sweetness of the tangy sauce in this dish make a great combination.

Heat the oil in a wok or large, nonstick frying pan. Add the aubergine chips and deep-fry for 1–2 minutes until golden. Remove and drain on kitchen paper.

Carefully pour off the oil to leave only 1 tablespoonful in the wok or pan. Quickly stir-fry the spring onions with the ginger and garlic, then mix in the soy sauce and chilli sauce. Add the aubergine chips and stir-fry for 1–2 minutes.

Mix the cornflour with a little water and then stir it into the mixture in the wok or pan. Cook until the sauce thickens then serve immediately.

Sir Patrick Moore's

selsey rarebit

PREP: 10 MINUTES
COOKING TIME: 5 MINUTES
SERVES: 2

2 thick slices of bread
15 g (½ oz) butter, softened
125 g (4 oz) mature Cheddar
 cheese
1–1½ tablespoons tomato
 ketchup
salt and pepper

Toast one side of the bread under a preheated grill until lightly browned.

Butter the other side of the bread and top with the cheese. Season with salt and pepper to taste.

Cook under the grill for 3–4 minutes until the cheese bubbles. Add a little tomato ketchup and eat.

❛ This book is helping people touched by breast cancer who need support and is a brilliant way to spend your money. ❜

> Here is a recipe for Welsh rarebit –
> or "rabbit" as it is commonly called –
> as I consider myself to be a Welsh
> Rarebit! With my best wishes.

Gemma Jones's
welsh rarebit

PREP: 8–10 MINUTES
COOKING TIME: 5 MINUTES
SERVES: 1

1 thick slice of bread
50 g (2 oz) mature Cheddar
    cheese, grated
1 teaspoon English mustard
    powder
½ onion, coarsely chopped
about 1 tablespoon milk

Toast the bread on one side under a preheated grill.

Mix together the cheese, mustard powder, onion and milk in a bowl. Spread on to the untoasted side of the toast.

Put the rarebit under a preheated hot grill until bubbly and brown. That's it – delicious!

red fruit coulis

PREP: 10 MINUTES, PLUS COOLING
NO COOK
SERVES: 6–8

3 tablespoons caster sugar

500 g (1 lb) ripe summer fruits,
    such as strawberries,
    raspberries and redcurrants

2–3 teaspoons lemon juice

Two or three summer fruits, blended and strained to a smooth and colourful purée, make a useful sauce for setting off all sorts of summer desserts. Use this coulis to flood the serving plates or drizzle it around the edges.

Put the sugar in a measuring jug and make it up to 50 ml (3½ fl oz) with boiling water. Stir until the sugar dissolves and leave to cool.

Remove the redcurrants (if used) from their stalks by running them through the tines of a fork. Place all the fruits in a food processor or blender and blend to a smooth purée, scraping the mixture down from the sides of the bowl if necessary. Blend in the sugar syrup.

Pour the sauce into a sieve set over a bowl. Press the purée with the back of a large metal spoon to squeeze out all the juice.

Stir in enough lemon juice to make the sauce slightly tangy, then transfer it to a jug. To serve, pour a little coulis on to each serving plate and gently tilt the plate so it is covered in an even layer. Alternatively, use a spoon to drizzle the sauce in a ribbon around the edges.

> ❝ I use this recipe for parties or just as a treat for family and friends. It is very easy to make and tastes just divine. It was a great comfort food for me during treatment and a nice treat for visitors! ❞
> **Sue Smith**, touched by breast cancer

cheat's
cheesecake ✿

PREP: 20 MINUTES, PLUS CHILLING
NO COOK
SERVES: 6–8

150 g (5 oz) digestive biscuits,
    crushed
50 g (2 oz) butter or margarine,
    melted
1 packet strawberry jelly
200 g (7 oz) full-fat cream cheese
caster sugar to taste, about
    3 tablespoons
150 ml (¼ pint) double cream
100 g (3½ oz) fresh strawberries,
    lightly mashed

Lightly oil a loose-based, 20 cm (8 inch) cake tin. Mix together the biscuit crumbs and butter or margarine and press the mixture into the base of the tin.

Make up the jelly with as little boiling water as possible to melt the cubes. When the cubes have dissolved, make it up to 300 ml (½ pint) with cold water and leave until cool but not setting.

Beat the cream cheese, adding sugar to taste, until it is soft and smooth. Whisk the cream until it stands in soft peaks. Stir in the mashed strawberries.

Mix the cooled jelly with the cream cheese, adding a little jelly at a time until it is combined. Gently mix in the whisked cream mixture. Pour over the biscuit base and place in the refrigerator for at least 2 hours to set.

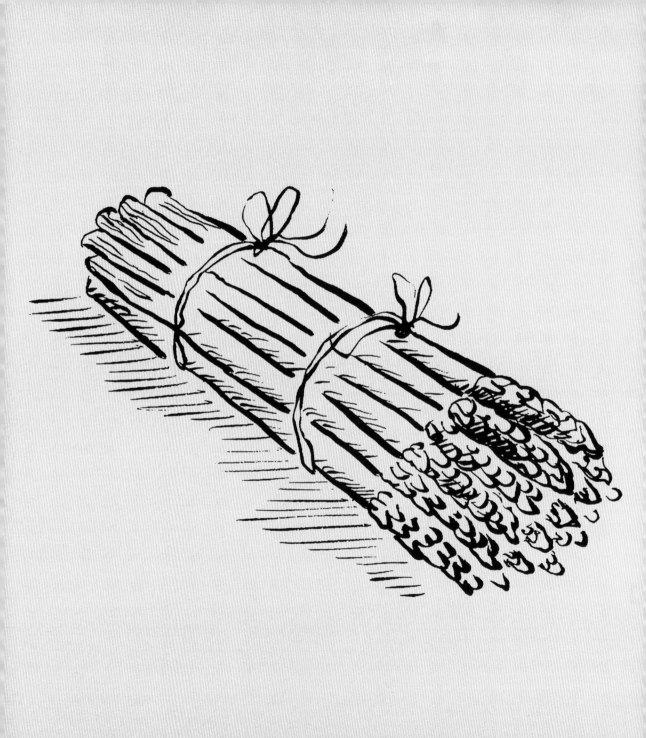

simply veggie

These dishes are so appetising that vegetarians and meat-eaters alike will be clamouring for second helpings. Here you'll find ideas for fresh summer lunches, such as *Onion Tarte Tatin,* and winter warmers like *Roasted Garlic Mash.* Or if you fancy a night in with a curry, try making your own *Red Thai Curry with Tofu.*

Ursula Ferrigno's
gnocchi di patate
(potato gnocchi)

" There are so many imitations ready prepared for us to buy, that I urge you to spend some time making gnocchi yourself. The results are infinitely superior, and it's certainly not difficult – in fact, it's fun! We use old potatoes here, rather than the waxy new ones, because the starch is fully developed and therefore allows the gnocchi to cohere. The gnocchi are also lighter in texture. The classical way to enjoy potato gnocchi is with a homemade tomato sauce. "

PREP: 30 MINUTES, PLUS COOLING
COOKING TIME: ABOUT
50 MINUTES
SERVES: 4

Gnocchi
250–300 g (8–10 oz) Italian '00'
    plain flour
2 small eggs
1 kg (2 lb) even-sized old
    potatoes, such as Maris Piper,
    King Edward or Desirée
sea salt
50 g (2 oz) unsalted softened
    butter, cubed
freshly grated Parmesan, to serve

Tomato sauce
500 g (1 lb) ripe tomatoes or
    400 g (13 oz) can Italian plum
    tomatoes
1 tablespoon olive oil
1 small onion, finely chopped
1 garlic clove, crushed
150 ml (¼ pint) vegetable stock or
    water
1 tablespoon tomato purée
pinch of caster sugar
handful of fresh basil leaves
    (optional), torn
sea salt and pepper
1 tablespoon dry white wine

Make the sauce. If you are using fresh tomatoes put them in a bowl, cover with boiling water for 30 seconds then plunge into cold water. Use a sharp knife to peel off the skins, cut them in half, discard the seeds and roughly chop the flesh.

Heat the oil in a saucepan, add the onion and cook gently for 5 minutes until softened. Add the tomatoes and garlic, cover and cook over a gentle heat, stirring occasionally, for 10 minutes.

Add the stock or water, tomato purée, sugar and basil (if used). Season to taste with salt and pepper. Half-cover the pan and simmer, stirring occasionally, for 20 minutes.

Sieve the tomato mixture into a clean pan. Bring to the boil, add the wine and keep to one side, off the heat.

Meanwhile, make the gnocchi. Cook the potatoes in their skins in boiling water for 20 minutes (or longer, depending on size) until tender. Drain well and, when they are cool enough to handle, peel off the skins. Mash until smooth. Leave to cool.

Sieve the flour into a bowl then mix with the potato and make a well in the centre. Crack the eggs into the well and mix. Knead to make a firm dough.

Cut the dough into pieces and use the palm of your hand to roll each piece into a long sausage shape. Cut them into 2.5 cm (1 inch) pieces. Flatten each piece slightly using a floured fork.

Cook the gnocchi a few at a time in salted boiling water, lifting them out with a slotted spoon as soon as they rise to the surface. Dot with butter and toss in the sauce. Serve with grated Parmesan.

red thai curry

with tofu and mixed vegetables

PREP: 20 MINUTES
COOKING TIME: 18–23 MINUTES
SERVES: 2

1 tablespoon rapeseed or olive oil

2 tablespoons red curry paste

1–2 fresh green chillies, deseeded
    and sliced

200 ml (7 fl oz) can light coconut
    milk

250 ml (8 fl oz) vegetable stock

1 large aubergine, diced

12 baby sweetcorn

100 g (3½ oz) mangetout

100 g (3½ oz) carrots, sliced

125 g (4 oz) fresh shiitake
    mushrooms, halved

1 large green pepper, cored,
    deseeded and sliced

150 g (5 oz) canned sliced
    bamboo shoots, drained

1 tablespoon soy sauce

1 tablespoon clear honey

2 kaffir lime leaves

400 g (13 oz) packet silken firm
    tofu, cubed

Heat the oil in a large saucepan and fry the curry paste and chillies for 1 minute, then stir in 2 tablespoons coconut milk (from the thicker part at the top of the can) and cook, stirring constantly, for 2 minutes.

Add the vegetable stock and bring to the boil. Toss in the aubergine, then bring the mixture back to the boil and simmer for about 5 minutes. Add the remaining vegetables and cook for another 5–10 minutes. Stir in the soy sauce, honey, lime leaves and the remaining coconut milk and simmer for another 5 minutes, stirring occasionally. Add the tofu cubes and mix well.

Serve the curry with steamed rice, torn Thai basil leaves and toasted cashew nuts, if liked.

> **"** This was the snack I missed while I was fighting breast cancer five years ago, and it is the one I prepared again and again after the treatment was over. **"**
> **Shila Sampat**, touched by breast cancer

potato vurra ✽

PREP: 25 MINUTES
COOKING TIME: 32 MINUTES
MAKES: 12–15 BALLS

700 g (2 lb) medium-large
   potatoes, peeled and chopped
1 teaspoon salt
2 teaspoons sugar
2 tablespoons lemon juice
½ teaspoon garam masala
1 teaspoon red chilli powder
1 tablespoon spring garlic leaves
   or coriander, chopped
vegetable oil, for deep-frying

Batter
225 g (7½ oz) yellow gram flour
1 tablespoon oil
1 teaspoon salt
½ teaspoon yellow turmeric powder

Put the potatoes in a pan of lightly salted boiling water and cook for 15 minutes, then drain. Mash and mix in the salt, sugar, lemon juice, garam masala, chilli powder and garlic leaves.

Use you hands to roll the mixture into 12–15 balls. Put them to one side.

Make the batter. Mix the flour, oil, salt and turmeric powder with about 300 ml (½ pint) water to make a thick but runny batter. Put 5 balls at a time in the batter.

Deep-fry the balls in batches for 4–5 minutes in a wok or deep frying pan over medium heat. Serve immediately with a green coriander chutney made by blending a handful of coriander leaves with a sliced green chilli, 2 tablespoons of desiccated coconut and salt, sugar and lemon juice to taste in a food processor or blender.

red rice pilaf

with fruit and nuts

PREP: 25 MINUTES
COOKING TIME: ABOUT
50 MINUTES
SERVES: 4

50 g (2 oz) wild rice

10 cardamom pods

2 teaspoons cumin seeds

2 teaspoons fennel seeds

4 tablespoons olive oil

25 g (1 oz) flaked almonds

2 red onions, thinly sliced

1 teaspoon caster sugar

½ teaspoon ground turmeric

2 garlic cloves, thinly sliced

250 g (8 oz) red rice

600 ml (1 pint) vegetable stock

25 g (1 oz) fresh root ginger,
   grated

6 tablespoons chopped parsley

75 g (3 oz) dried apricots, thinly
   sliced

250 g (8 oz) ricotta cheese

salt and pepper

Bring a saucepan of lightly salted water to the boil. Add the wild rice and cook gently for 25–30 minutes or until tender.

Crush the cardamom pods using a pestle and mortar to release the seeds. Discard the shells, then add the cumin and fennel seeds and crush lightly.

Meanwhile, heat half the oil in a large frying pan, add the almonds and fry gently, stirring, until lightly browned. Remove with a slotted spoon. Add the remaining oil, onions and sugar to the pan and fry gently for 5 minutes until golden. Lift out half the onions and fry the remainder until crisp. Transfer to kitchen paper and reserve for sprinkling.

Return the lightly cooked onions to the pan with the crushed spices, turmeric and garlic and fry, stirring, for 1 minute. Add the rice and stock and bring to the boil. Reduce the heat, cover with a lid or foil and cook gently for 25–30 minutes or until the rice is tender, adding a little more water if the stock runs dry.

Stir in the ginger, parsley and apricots and check the seasoning. Dot with teaspoonfuls of ricotta and fold in gently. Pile the pilaf on to plates and serve scattered with the crisp onions and fried almonds.

felafel

PREP: 10 MINUTES
COOKING TIME: 6 MINUTES
SERVES: 4

425 g (14 oz) can chickpeas,
   rinsed and drained
1 onion, roughly chopped
3 garlic cloves, roughly chopped
2 teaspoons cumin seeds
1 teaspoon mild chilli powder
2 tablespoons chopped mint
3 tablespoons chopped coriander
50 g (2 oz) breadcrumbs
vegetable oil, for frying
salt and pepper

These spicy chickpea cakes make a great vegetarian supper served simply with a salad and pitta breads.

Put the chickpeas in a blender or food processor with the onion, garlic, spices, herbs, breadcrumbs and a little salt and pepper. Blend to make a chunky paste.

Take dessertspoonfuls of the mixture and flatten into round cakes. Heat oil to a depth of 1 cm (½ inch) in a frying pan and fry half the falafel for about 3 minutes, turning once, until crisp and golden. Drain on kitchen paper and keep warm while you cook the remainder.

stir-fried spicy
tempeh
with vegetables

PREP: 15 MINUTES
COOKING TIME: ABOUT
10 MINUTES
SERVES: 2

1 tablespoon rapeseed or olive oil

2 fresh red chillies, sliced

2 lemon grass stalks, finely sliced

2 kaffir lime leaves

1 large garlic clove, crushed

2 slices fresh root ginger, peeled
   and chopped

1 tablespoon tamarind paste

2 tablespoons vegetable stock

2 teaspoons shoyu or tamari
   sauce

1 tablespoon clear honey

500 g (1 lb) tempeh, cut into
   strips

125 g (4 oz) baby sweetcorn

125 g (4 oz) asparagus, halved

Heat the oil in a nonstick sauté pan or wok over a high heat until piping hot. Swirl it around the pan then add the chillies, lemon grass, lime leaves, garlic and ginger. Turn the heat down to medium and stir-fry the spices for about 2–3 minutes.

Add the tamarind, vegetable stock, shoyu or tamari sauce and honey and cook for about 2–3 minutes until the sauce is thick and glossy.

Add the tempeh, sweetcorn and asparagus and stir-fry for about 2 minutes to warm them through.

> ❛This is a very simple and lightly spiced dish, quick to cook and great to eat. It was my favourite during my treatment and recovery from breast cancer and helped to cheer me up every time.❜
> **Snober Bhangu MBE**, **Breast Cancer Care volunteer, diagnosed 2000**

achari aloo ✱

PREP: 15 MINUTES
COOKING TIME: 50 MINUTES
SERVES: 4

2 tablespoons olive oil
2 onions, finely chopped
½ teaspoon whole cumin seeds
2 large tomatoes, finely chopped
1 teaspoon curry powder
6 large potatoes, peeled and
    quartered
2 tablespoons mango pickle or
    chutney
salt
naan bread, to serve

To garnish
chopped fresh coriander
½ teaspoon garam masala

Mango pickle is widely available in most supermarkets and Indian grocery shops.

Heat the oil in a large, heavy-based saucepan and fry the onions for 7–8 minutes, stirring continuously, until they turn golden-brown. Add the cumin seeds and fry for 20 seconds.

Add the tomatoes and stir until the mixture turns into a smooth paste and the oil just begins to separate.

Season with the curry powder and salt to taste. Add the potatoes and 50 ml (2 fl oz) water. Cover the pan and leave on a low heat for 40–45 minutes until the potatoes are tender and the mixture is fairly dry.

Chop any large pieces in the mango pickle or chutney and add the pickle to the potatoes. Serve immediately, garnished with coriander and garam masala and accompanied with naan bread.

buckwheat
noodles

PREP: 15 MINUTES
COOKING TIME: 15 MINUTES
SERVES: 2

250 g (8 oz) tofu

2 tablespoons vegetable oil

3 garlic cloves, crushed

1 hot red chilli, deseeded and
    chopped

1 bunch of spring onions, sliced
    into 1.5 cm (¾ inch) lengths

100 g (3½ oz) mangetout, each
    sliced into 3 pieces

300 g (10 oz) pumpkin, deseeded,
    skinned and cut into 5 mm x 5
    cm (¼ x 2 inch) sticks

150 g (5 oz) buckwheat noodles

Dressing

½ teaspoon cornflour

4 tablespoons mirin

1 tablespoon caster sugar

1 tablespoon (1 sachet) miso
    soup paste

2 tablespoons toasted sesame oil

2 tablespoons light soy sauce

Make the dressing by blending the cornflour with 1 tablespoon water in a small bowl. Add the mirin, sugar, miso paste, sesame oil and soy sauce and stir to mix.

Bring a large saucepan of lightly salted water to the boil, ready to cook the noodles. Drain the tofu, pat it dry on kitchen paper and cut it into small chunks.

Heat the oil in a large frying pan or wok. Add the garlic and chilli and fry for 15 seconds. Add the tofu, spring onions, mangetout and pumpkin and stir-fry for 8–10 minutes or until the vegetables have softened but retain a little texture.

Meanwhile, cook the noodles in the water for about 10 minutes or until tender. Drain through a colander and tip into the pan with the vegetables and tofu.

Stir the dressing, add it to the pan and cook it for 1 minute, tossing the ingredients together until heated through. Serve immediately.

pasta primavera

PREP: 20 MINUTES
COOKING TIME: 20 MINUTES
SERVES: 4

100 g (3½ oz) baby carrots
125 g (4 oz) fresh broad beans
150 g (5 oz) fresh peas
200 g (7 oz) asparagus tips
25 g (1 oz) butter
1 fennel bulb or 4 baby fennel,
    thinly sliced
275 g (9 oz) fresh tagliatelle or
    pappardelle
300 ml (½ pint) double cream
3 tablespoons pesto
salt and pepper
Parmesan cheese, freshly grated,
    to serve

This is a great recipe to make with spring vegetables. This version has a little pesto stirred into the sauce, giving it a lift without detracting from the fresh flavours of the vegetables.

Bring a large saucepan of lightly salted water to the boil and cook the carrots for 3 minutes or until softened. Add the beans and peas to the pan and cook for a further 2–3 minutes or until just tender. Add the asparagus tips and cook for a further 1 minute. Lift out all the vegetables with a slotted spoon, reserving the water.

Melt the butter in a large frying pan and gently fry the sliced fennel for 5 minutes.

Return the vegetable water to the boil and add the pasta. Bring back to the boil and cook for 1–2 minutes or according to the packet instructions until tender. Drain the pasta and return it to the pan.

Add the cream, pesto and a little salt and pepper to the frying pan and heat through for a couple of minutes. Tip the sauce into the pasta pan with all the vegetables and toss together. Pile on to warm serving plates and serve sprinkled with grated Parmesan.

focaccia
sandwich

PREP: 20 MINUTES
COOKING TIME: 20 MINUTES
SERVES: 4

2 red peppers
1 small aubergine, sliced
2 courgettes, sliced lengthways
1 red onion, sliced into rings
1 focaccia loaf
1 garlic clove, halved (optional)
150 g (5 oz) mozzarella cheese,
    sliced
75 g (3 oz) rocket
olive oil, to drizzle
salt and pepper

Heat a griddle pan and griddle the red peppers, whole, until the skins are charred. Set aside to cool.

Griddle the aubergine, courgettes and onion for about 5 minutes, turning occasionally. Leave to cool.

Cut the focaccia in half horizontally and place each half on the griddle and toast lightly. Rub the cut edges of the garlic (if used) over the toasted bread. Place the sliced mozzarella on the bottom of the toasted focaccia.

Remove and discard the skin from the cooled griddled peppers and deseed. Chop the flesh roughly.

Layer the griddled vegetables evenly on top of the mozzarella. Start with the aubergine, then add the courgettes, red peppers, onion and the rocket. Season each layer as you arrange it.

Drizzle a little olive oil over the vegetables, season to taste and place the top of the focaccia bread on top of the vegetables. Push together gently but firmly, cut into 4 equal pieces and serve.

$\mathcal{L}$otte Duncan's
blue cheese, walnut and red onion soda bread

PREP: 20 MINUTES, PLUS COOLING
COOKING TIME: 30 MINUTES
SERVES: 6

1 tablespoon olive oil

1 red onion, sliced

50 g (2 oz) walnut halves

125 g (4 oz) Stilton cheese, crumbled

175 g (6 oz) plain white flour

175 g (6 oz) plain wholemeal flour

125 g (4 oz) coarse oatmeal

2 teaspoons bicarbonate of soda

1 teaspoon salt

1 teaspoon honey

300 ml (½ pint) buttermilk

2–3 tablespoons milk

Heat the oil in a frying pan, add the onion and cook gently for 10 minutes. Remove the pan from the heat and add the walnut halves, then stir in the cheese. Leave to cool.

Combine all the dry ingredients in a large bowl. Make a well in the centre, toss in the onion mixture and gradually beat in the honey, buttermilk and enough milk to form a soft dough. Turn on to a lightly floured surface and knead for about 5 minutes until smooth. Shape into a round and cut a deep cross on the top with a knife.

Place the loaf on a floured baking sheet and bake in a preheated oven, 200°C (400°F), Gas Mark 6, for about 30 minutes or until the bread is slightly risen and sounds hollow when tapped.

roast vegetable and
feta tart

PREP: 25 MINUTES, PLUS CHILLING
COOKING TIME: 45 MINUTES
SERVES: 6

Pastry

125 g (4 oz) self-raising flour

50 g (2 oz) oatmeal

75 g (3 oz) chilled butter, diced

Filling

1 aubergine, sliced

1 red pepper, cored, deseeded
   and cut into thick strips

1 onion, cut into wedges

2 courgettes, cut into thick slices

3 tomatoes, halved

2 garlic cloves, chopped

3 tablespoons olive oil

4 small rosemary sprigs

125 g (4 oz) feta cheese,
   crumbled

2 tablespoons grated Parmesan
   cheese

salt and pepper

Feta cheese, the best known Greek cheese, is made from ewes' milk. Its distinctive flavour goes well with these Mediterranean vegetables.

Make the pastry. Mix the flour and oatmeal, then rub in the butter. Add 3 tablespoons cold water and mix to a firm dough. Knead briefly, then chill for 30 minutes.

Make the filling. Mix all the vegetables in a roasting tin. Add the garlic, oil and rosemary and season to taste with salt and pepper. Turn the mixture to coat the vegetables evenly and roast in a preheated oven, 200°C (400°F), Gas Mark 6, for 35 minutes.

Meanwhile, roll out the pastry on a lightly floured surface and use it to line a 23 cm (9 inch) ovenproof dish. Bake blind in the preheated oven for 15 minutes. Remove the paper and beans or foil and return to the oven for 5 minutes.

Fill the pastry case with the vegetables, arrange the feta on top and sprinkle with Parmesan. Return the tart to the oven for 10 minutes and serve warm or cold.

ratatouille

PREP: 25 MINUTES
COOKING TIME: 45 MINUTES
SERVES: 6

150 ml (¼ pint) olive oil

1 kg (2 lb) well-flavoured
   tomatoes, skinned and roughly
   chopped

½ teaspoon caster sugar

2 teaspoons chopped rosemary
   or thyme

2 onions, thinly sliced

3 red or yellow peppers, or a
   mixture of the two, deseeded
   and cut into small chunks

1 large aubergine, about 400 g
   (13 oz), halved lengthways and
   thinly sliced

2 courgettes, sliced

3 garlic cloves, chopped

salt and pepper

This Provençal vegetable stew can be served hot or cold and cooked to a firm or soft consistency, depending on personal preference. It also reheats well if you want to make it a day in advance.

Heat half the oil in a saucepan, add the tomatoes, sugar, herbs and a little salt and pepper and fry gently, stirring frequently, for about 10 minutes or until the tomatoes are soft. Raise the temperature and cook quickly for about 5 minutes until the mixture has thickened.

Fry the onions in the remaining oil in a separate, large saucepan or frying pan for about 5 minutes or until softened. Add the peppers and aubergines and fry gently, stirring, for 5 minutes. Stir in the courgettes and garlic and fry for a further 5 minutes.

Combine the 2 mixtures, using whichever pan is the larger. Cook gently for about 15 minutes or until the vegetables are tender but retain a little texture. Check the seasoning and serve.

bruschetta

PREP: 10 MINUTES, PLUS
STANDING
COOKING TIME: 5 MINUTES
SERVES: 4

400 g (13 oz) very ripe tomatoes,
    finely chopped
2 tablespoons extra virgin olive
    oil
4 slices of crusty bread
1 large garlic clove, unpeeled
salt

In the height of summer, when tomatoes are at their sweetest and juiciest, this poor man's dish becomes the most divine crowd pleaser.

Put the tomatoes in a bowl, season with salt and stir in the oil. Set aside for at least 15 minutes for the salt to draw out the tomato juices.

Grill the bread on both sides under a preheated very hot grill, with the rack about 8 cm (3 inches) from the heat, until it is crisp and lightly charred around the edges. Alternatively, griddle or barbecue the bread.

Rub one side of each slice with the garlic clove (the skin will break as you start rubbing it against the bread), then lay the bread, garlic side up, on a platter. Top with the chopped tomatoes, making sure that you include the tasty juices, and serve.

> ❛ I'm honoured to have worked on this project, to have spoken to inspiring volunteers and to have been part of celebrating one of life's pleasures and one of my favourite things – food! ❜
> **Sara Donaldson**, **Breast Cancer Care employee**

aubergine
bake ✳

PREP: 20 MINUTES
COOKING TIME: 45 MINUTES
SERVES: 6

2 tablespoons olive oil

2 aubergines, sliced

1 onion, finely chopped

2 x 400 g (13 oz) cans chopped
    tomatoes

1 tablespoon tomato purée

1–2 garlic cloves, finely chopped

1 teaspoon dried oregano

1 tablespoon fresh basil,
    chopped

250 g (8 oz) buffalo mozzarella,
    drained and sliced

25 g (1 oz) Parmesan cheese,
    freshly grated

salt and pepper

Heat 1 tablespoon of the oil in a large frying pan and fry the aubergine slices until they are brown on both sides. Drain and set aside.

Fry the onion gently in the remaining oil for 5 minutes or until softened. Then add the tomatoes, tomato purée, garlic, oregano and basil, stirring to make sauce. Season to taste with salt and pepper and simmer uncovered for about 10 minutes to reduce and thicken.

Beginning with aubergines, layer the aubergines, sauce and mozzarella in a 1.2 litre (2 pint) ovenproof dish, repeating until all the ingredients are used.

Scatter the Parmesan on top and bake in a preheated oven, 190°C (375°F), Gas Mark 5, for about 30 minutes until bubbling.

onion tarte tatin

PREP: 30 MINUTES, PLUS CHILLING
COOKING TIME: 40–50 MINUTES
SERVES 4–6

Pastry

175 g (6 oz) self-raising
   wholemeal flour

75 g (3 oz) chilled butter, diced

2 tablespoons chopped parsley

2 teaspoons chopped thyme

2–3 tablespoons lemon juice

Filling

500 g (1 lb) shallots, peeled

25 g (1 oz) butter

2 tablespoons olive oil

2 teaspoons muscovado sugar

salt and pepper

Shallots are related to onions but form a cluster of small bulbs rather than a single one. They have a more subtle flavour than onions and are not as pungent as garlic.

Sift the flour into a bowl and rub in the butter until the mixture resembles breadcrumbs. Stir in the herbs and lemon juice and mix to a firm dough. Knead briefly, then chill for 30 minutes.

Make the filling. Boil the shallots for 10 minutes and drain well. Heat the butter and oil in an ovenproof frying pan and gently fry the shallots, stirring, for about 10 minutes or until they start to colour. Sprinkle over the sugar, season to taste with salt and pepper and cook gently for 5 minutes until well coloured.

Roll out the dough on a lightly floured surface to a circle a little larger than the pan. Support the dough on your rolling pin and lay it over the shallots, tucking the edges of the pastry down the side of the pan.

Bake the tart in a preheated oven, 200°C (400°F), Gas Mark 6, for 20–25 minutes until the pastry case is crisp. Leave the tart to cool for 5 minutes, then put a large plate over the pan and invert the tart on to it. Serve the tart warm or cold.

$\mathcal{R}$ula Lenska's
mama's avocado soup

PREP: 10 MINUTES
NO COOK
SERVES: 4

3 ripe avocados, peeled and
    stoned
1 teaspoon curry powder
300 ml (½ pint) vegetable stock
2 tablespoons lemon juice
125 ml (4 fl oz) double cream
1 tablespoon chopped parsley
salt and pepper

To garnish
chopped avocado
parsley sprigs
pumpernickel bread

Place all the ingredients together in a food processor or blender and blend until smooth. Heat gently in a saucepan if you wish to eat it hot, or serve cold.

Garnish with pieces of avocado and parsley and serve immediately (since avocado discolours so quickly) with strips of pumpernickel bread.

❛ I have recently lost a school friend to breast cancer and have another one who is undergoing treatment. I laud and support the wonderful work that Breast Cancer Care does. Good luck. ❜

parsnip and
potato rösti

PREP: 15 MINUTES
COOKING TIME: 15 MINUTES
SERVES: 4

500 g (1 lb) medium waxy
   potatoes
400 g (13 oz) small parsnips
2 garlic cloves, finely chopped
25 g (1 oz) butter
2–3 tablespoons olive oil
salt and pepper

These little potato cakes have a delicious texture because they're made using grated potato rather than mash. Sweet, young parsnips add plenty of flavour, and make the perfect accompaniment to beef, lamb or game dishes.

Cut the potatoes and parsnips into large chunks. Bring a large saucepan of lightly salted water to the boil, add the potatoes and cook for 2 minutes. Add the parsnips and cook for a further 3 minutes. Drain and leave until cool enough to handle.

Coarsely grate the vegetables and mix them together in a bowl. Sprinkle with the garlic and a little salt and pepper and mix together well. Divide the mixture into 4 portions and pat each into a flat cake between the palms of your hands.

Melt the butter with 2 tablespoon oil in a large frying pan. Add the potato cakes and fry gently for about 5 minutes or until golden on the underside. Turn them over and fry for a further 5 minutes, drizzling with a little more oil if the pan is very dry.

courgette and
boursin soup ❋

PREP: 10 MINUTES
COOKING TIME: 35 MINUTES
SERVES: 5–6

1 kg (2 lb) courgettes, thickly
   sliced
1 onion, chopped
600 ml (1 pint) vegetable stock
150 g (5 oz) Boursin cheese
300 ml (½ pint) single cream
salt and pepper
chopped chives, to garnish

Put the courgettes and onion in a large, heavy-based saucepan and add the stock. Bring to the boil and simmer for 30 minutes.

Leave the soup to cool, then transfer it to a blender or food processor and liquidize.

Reheat the soup gently and add the Boursin, stirring until melted. Add most of the cream and season to taste with salt and pepper.

Serve with a swirl of the remaining cream and garnished with chives.

roasted garlic

mash

PREP: 15 MINUTES
COOKING TIME: 45 MINUTES
SERVES: 4

6 garlic cloves, left unpeeled
2 tablespoons olive oil
1 tablespoon finely chopped
    rosemary or thyme
3 baking potatoes, about 750 g
    (1½ lb) in total, unpeeled and
    cut into small chunks
50 g (2 oz) butter
125 ml (4 fl oz) milk
salt and pepper

Put the garlic cloves in a small ovenproof dish. Drizzle with the oil and sprinkle with the herbs. Cover with foil and bake in a preheated oven, 160°C (325°F), Gas Mark 3, for 35–40 minutes or until they are soft.

Meanwhile, cook the potatoes in a large saucepan of boiling water for about 20 minutes or until tender.

Remove the garlic from the oven and, when it is cool, squeeze the cloves from their skins into a small bowl. Mash with a fork. Strain the oil from the dish through a sieve held over the garlic and mix well.

Combine the butter and milk in a small saucepan over a low heat and heat until the butter is melted. Drain the potatoes well when cooked, transfer to a warm bowl and mash well.

Add the butter mixture to the potatoes and stir until smooth. Stir in the mashed roasted garlic and season to taste with salt and pepper.

roasted
vegetables ✳

PREP: 30 MINUTES
COOKING TIME: 1 HOUR
SERVES: 6

1 small butternut squash, skin left
    on and seeds removed
1 sweet potato, peeled
1 aubergine
1 courgette
1 red pepper, cored and deseeded
6 asparagus spears
6 shallots, peeled
8 mushrooms
2 garlic cloves, chopped
1 tablespoon chopped thyme
2 tablespoons mixed seeds
6 tablespoons olive oil
250g (8 oz) haloumi cheese
pasta or rice, to serve

Cut the squash, sweet potato, aubergine, courgette, red pepper, asparagus spears, shallots and mushrooms into bite-sized pieces.

Put the vegetables into a baking tin with the garlic, mix together and sprinkle over the thyme and mixed seeds. Add the oil and use your hands to turn the vegetables until they are thoroughly coated.

Cook in a preheated oven, 180°C (350°F), Gas Mark 4, for 30 minutes or until the vegetables are soft. Slice the cheese and arrange it over the vegetables and cook for a further 30 minutes. Serve with pasta or rice.

❛ As the Practical Support Coordinator for Breast Cancer Care in the London & South Region I know that many people going through treatment are looking for recipes that are healthy and nutritious. This dish ticks both boxes and has the added advantages of being absolutely delicious and easy to prepare. Enjoy! ❜

Gill Swain-Coad,
Breast Cancer Care employee

girls' night in

There's nothing quite like a good old-fashioned girls' night. It's a great chance to gather your friends round for a good gossip and a bite to eat. The recipes in this chapter include classics such as the delicious *Rich Chocolate Cake*, as well as great ideas for pre-dinner snacks like *Roasted Paprika Potato Wedges*.

roasted paprika

potato wedges

PREP: 5 MINUTES
COOKING TIME: 35–40 MINUTES
SERVES: 4

4 large baking potatoes, about
250 g (8 oz) each, left unpeeled
4 tablespoons olive or sunflower
oil
1–2 teaspoons paprika
salt
soured cream mixed with chives,
or aïoli or mayonnaise, to serve

Scrub the potatoes well, rinse them under cold running water and pat dry with kitchen paper. Cut each potato lengthways into 8 wedges.

Place the potato wedges in a roasting tin, drizzle over the oil and toss well to coat. Sprinkle over the paprika and season with salt. Place the potatoes in the top of a preheated oven, 220°C (425°F), Gas Mark 7, and roast for 35–40 minutes, basting them with the oil 2–3 times during cooking, until they are tender and nicely browned.

Serve the wedges as a starter with a bowl of soured cream mixed with snipped chives, or with aïoli or mayonnaise, or as a side dish to replace traditional roast potatoes or chips.

Esther Rantzen's
fish pie

PREP: 30 MINUTES
COOKING TIME: ABOUT 1 HOUR
SERVES: 4

1 kg (2 lb) haddock or cod
600 ml (1 pint) milk
125 g (4 oz) butter
50 g (2 oz) flour
4 hard-boiled eggs, chopped
4 tablespoons chopped parsley
2 tablespoons lemon juice
salt and pepper
sprig of parsley, to garnish
green vegetables, to serve

Mashed potatoes
1 kg (2 lb) potatoes
150 ml (¼ pint) milk
50 g (2 oz) butter

Put the fish in shallow baking dish, pour over half the milk and bake for 15 minutes in a preheated oven, 200°C (400°F), Gas Mark 6.

Meanwhile, make a white sauce. Melt the butter in heavy-based saucepan and add the flour. Stir in the remaining milk together with the milk in which the fish was cooked. Season to taste with salt and pepper. Mix to a smooth consistency and cook for 2 minutes. Add the flaked fish to the sauce, together with the eggs, parsley and lemon juice.

Make the mashed potatoes. Cut the potatoes into large pieces and cook in lightly salted boiling water for about 15 minutes. Drain and mash well with the milk and butter.

Put the fish mixture into a 1.5 litre (2½ pint) baking dish and spoon the potatoes over the top. Bake the pie in a preheated oven, 200°C (400°F), Gas Mark 6, for about 30 minutes, until the top is golden brown.

vegetable crisps

with tomato salsa

PREP: 20 MINUTES
COOKING TIME: ABOUT
15 MINUTES
SERVES: 4

Vegetable crisps
250 g (8 oz) potato
250 g (8 oz) parsnip
250 g (8 oz) beetroot
vegetable oil, for deep-frying
salt and pepper

Tomato salsa
6 small ripe tomatoes, skinned
and finely chopped
1–2 red or green chillies,
deseeded and finely chopped
2 tablespoons finely chopped
onion
2 tablespoons chopped fresh
coriander
2 tablespoons lime juice
2 teaspoons vinegar
¼ teaspoon salt

Use a sharp knife to cut the vegetables into as thin slices as you can manage. Pat them dry on kitchen paper.

Pour the oil into a large saucepan until it is about one-third full. Heat the oil until a piece of vegetable sizzles on the surface. Add a batch of vegetable slices to the oil and fry until crisp and golden.

Remove the vegetables and drain on kitchen paper while you fry the rest in batches (do not add too many pieces at once or they will go soggy). Sprinkle with salt and pepper.

Make the salsa by putting all the ingredients into a blender or food processor and blend until smooth. Season to taste with pepper and serve with the crisps.

bean nachos

with melted cheese

PREP: 10 MINUTES
COOKING TIME: 10 MINUTES
SERVES: 4

225 g (7½ oz) tortilla chips
420 g (13½ oz) can baked beans
1 avocado
200 g (7 oz) cherry tomatoes,
   halved
125 g (4 oz) Cheddar cheese,
   grated
1 large green chilli, finely sliced
pepper

Put the tortilla chips in a large, heatproof serving dish or 4 smaller serving dishes. Spoon the baked beans over the chips.

Peel the avocado, remove the stone and cut the flesh into dice. Arrange the tomatoes and avocado pieces over the beans, scatter over the Cheddar and top with the sliced chilli.

Season well with pepper and bake in a preheated oven, 200°C (400°F), Gas Mark 6, for 10 minutes or until the cheese is bubbling and the tops of the nachos have browned.

pasta puttanesca

PREP: 10 MINUTES
COOKING TIME: ABOUT
30 MINUTES
SERVES: 4

4 tablespoons olive oil

2 onions, chopped

2 garlic cloves, finely chopped

8 anchovy fillets, coarsely
    chopped

400 g (13 oz) can plum tomatoes,
    drained and roughly chopped

12 black olives, pitted and halved

1 tablespoon capers, drained

2 tablespoons chopped oregano

300 g (10 oz) fusilli or other dried
    pasta shapes

125 g (4 oz) freshly grated
    Parmesan cheese

salt and pepper

red basil leaves, to garnish

Heat the oil in a saucepan over a moderate heat, add the onions and cook gently for 5–10 minutes until softened. Add the garlic and anchovies and cook for a further 3 minutes or until the anchovies disintegrate into the sauce.

Stir in the tomatoes, olives, capers and oregano and season to taste with salt and pepper. Simmer the sauce gently for about 20 minutes, stirring occasionally.

Meanwhile, bring a large saucepan of lightly salted water to the boil and plunge in the pasta. Bring the water back to the boil and simmer for 8–10 minutes or according to the instructions on the packet until it is tender but firm to the bite.

Drain the pasta thoroughly, then toss it with the sauce. Serve immediately, sprinkled with the Parmesan and garnished with basil.

> " I shared this recipe with my husband and daughter when we returned from the clinic in which we received the results of my surgery. "
>
> **Jenny Jones**, Breast Cancer Care volunteer, diagnosed 2006

mediterranean
pasta bake ✽

PREP: 25 MINUTES
COOKING TIME: 50 MINUTES
SERVES: 4–6

1 aubergine or 2 courgettes

3 tablespoons olive oil, plus extra
    for drizzling

1 onion, chopped

1 red and 1 green pepper, cored,
    deseeded and diced

1 bunch of basil, chopped

2 x 400 g (13 oz) cans chopped
    tomatoes

300 g (10 oz) pasta shapes

25 g (1 oz) of pitted black olives

200 ml (7 fl oz) crème fraîche

1 egg, beaten

150 g (5 oz) feta or mozzarella
    cheese, diced

salt and pepper

Cut the aubergine or courgettes in slices 1 cm (½ inch) thick. Place them on a lightly oiled baking sheet, drizzle over 2 tablespoons of oil and bake in a preheated oven, 180°C (350°F), Gas Mark 4, for about 20 minutes.

Meanwhile, heat the remaining oil in a large frying pan and fry the onion and peppers for about 5 minutes. Add half the basil and cook for a further 5 minutes. Add the tomatoes to the pan, season to taste with salt and pepper and simmer for 10 minutes. Cook the pasta in lightly salted boiling water as directed on the packet. Drain.

Dice the cooked aubergine or courgette slices and stir into the tomato mixture. Stir in the cooked pasta and transfer to a ovenproof casserole dish. Scatter the remaining basil and the olives over the top.

Mix together the crème fraîche, egg and cheese and pour evenly over the pasta. Bake at the same oven temperature for 30 minutes or until the topping is slightly browned. Serve with a green salad and some warm bread, if liked.

salmon tart

with wholegrain mustard and rocket

PREP: 20 MINUTES, PLUS CHILLING
COOKING TIME: 45–50 MINUTES
SERVES: 4

Pastry

225 g (7½ oz) plain flour

100 g (3½ oz) butter

grated rind of 1 lemon

1 tablespoon cracked black
   pepper

Filling

300 g (10 oz) salmon fillet or loin,
   skinned and all bones removed

250 ml (8 fl oz) milk

50 g (2 oz) rocket, chopped, plus
   extra leaves to garnish

3 eggs, beaten

3 tablespoons wholegrain
   mustard

5 spring onions, finely chopped

Put the flour, butter, lemon rind and black pepper in a food processor and blitz until the mixture resembles fine breadcrumbs. Add 4 tablespoons iced water and pulse a few times until the mixture comes together. Cover with clingfilm and chill for 1 hour.

Roll out the pastry on a lightly floured surface and use it to line a deep 20 cm (8 inch) fluted tart tin. Chill the pastry case for 30 minutes, then bake blind in a preheated oven, 200°C (400°F), Gas Mark 6, for 15 minutes. Remove the paper and beans or foil and return it to the oven for a further 5 minutes. Leave the oven on.

Meanwhile, poach the salmon in the milk for 5 minutes until cooked. Leave to cool slightly. Put the chopped rocket in the pastry case. Remove the salmon from the milk and strain, reserving the cooking liquid. Break the salmon into bite-sized pieces and arrange them over the rocket.

Beat together the eggs, mustard, spring onions and poaching milk and pour over the salmon. Bake in the oven for 25–30 minutes until golden and firm. Garnish with rocket leaves.

garlic prawn

tapas

PREP TIME: 10 MINUTES
COOKING TIME: 10 MINUTES
SERVES: 4

2 garlic cloves, crushed

1 teaspoon paprika

1 medium-hot red chilli,
    deseeded and finely chopped

2 tablespoons extra virgin olive
    oil

500 g (1 lb) raw whole large
    prawns

salt

aïoli, to serve

These spice-coated prawns taste so good that they are worthy of a main meal, served with plenty of tasty bread and other little nibbles. If you're entertaining, prepare everything in advance and keep in the refrigerator, well covered, until you're ready to cook.

Mix together the garlic, paprika, chilli, oil and a little salt in a large bowl. (If you are preparing this dish in advance, leave the salt until you're ready to cook.)

Add the prawns to the bowl and toss them in the mixture until they are evenly coated.

Heat a ridged grill pan or heavy-based frying pan and add half the prawns, spreading them in a single layer. Cook for 2–3 minutes or until they are deep pink on the underside. Turn them over and cook for a further 1–2 minutes. Transfer the prawns to a warm dish and cook the remainder in the same way. Serve with aïoli.

Nigel Havers'
hamburger holstein

" Cancer used to be seen as a death sentence, but thanks to the wonderful work done by all the medical profession, we are making enormous progress and slowly but surely beating this disease – it is for this reason that we must all step up our support for both research and care and work together to make the word cancer become nothing but a memory. "

PREP: 15 MINUTES
COOKING TIME: 8–12 MINUTES
SERVES: 6

1 kg (2 lb) chuck steak, cubed
1 small red onion
1 tablespoon roughly chopped
    parsley
1 teaspoon double cream
1 tablespoon freshly grated
    Parmesan cheese
4 tablespoons oil
6 eggs
12 anchovy fillets
salt and pepper
green salad, to serve

Put the steak, onion and parsley in a food processor and process until minced. Add the cream and Parmesan and season with salt and pepper. Mix together, then form into 6 burgers.

Heat 2 tablespoons of the oil in large frying pan, add the burgers and cook quickly over a high heat to sear on both sides. Turn down the heat and cook for 4–6 minutes, depending how well done you like your meat. Remove from the pan and keep warm.

Using a clean pan, fry the eggs in the remaining oil and place them on top of the burgers. Arrange 2 anchovy fillets on top of each and serve with a green salad.

bolognese sauce

PREP: 15 MINUTES
COOKING TIME: 1 HOUR
SERVES: 4

15 g (½ oz) butter

3 tablespoons olive oil

1 large onion, finely chopped

1 celery stick, finely chopped

1 carrot, finely chopped

3 garlic cloves, crushed

500 g (1 lb) lean minced beef

150 ml (¼ pint) red wine

2 x 400 g (13 oz) cans chopped
   tomatoes

2 tablespoons sun-dried tomato
   paste

3 tablespoons chopped oregano

3 bay leaves

salt and pepper

grated Parmesan cheese, to
   serve (optional)

Bolognese sauce is usually served with tagliatelle rather than spaghetti. It should be thick and pulpy, rather than thin and gravy-like, so it clings to the pasta.

Melt the butter with the oil in a large, heavy-based saucepan and gently fry the onion for 5 minutes. Add the celery and carrot and fry gently for a further 2 minutes.

Stir in the garlic, then add the minced beef. Fry gently, breaking up the meat, until lightly browned.

Add the wine and let the mixture bubble until the wine reduces slightly. Stir in the chopped tomatoes, tomato paste, oregano and bay leaves and bring to the boil.

Reduce the heat and cook very gently, uncovered, for about 45 minutes or until the sauce is very thick and pulpy. Check the seasoning, and serve with grated Parmesan, if liked.

lasagne

PREP: 25 MINUTES
COOKING TIME: 1 HOUR
SERVES: 4–5

200 g (7 oz) chicken livers

25 g (1 oz) butter

1 quantity Bolognese Sauce (see page 140)

75 g (3 oz) Parmesan cheese, freshly grated

150 g (5 oz) fresh or dried plain or spinach-flavoured lasagne

freshly grated nutmeg

salt and pepper

Béchamel sauce

50 g (2 oz) butter

40 g (1½ oz) plain flour

600 ml (1 pint) milk

freshly grated nutmeg

salt and pepper

Bring a large saucepan of salted water to the boil, ready to cook the pasta if using fresh. Rinse the chicken livers, pat them dry on kitchen paper and finely chop, discarding any fatty, white parts. Melt the butter in a small frying pan. Add the livers and a little salt and pepper and fry gently for 5 minutes. Stir into the bolognese sauce.

Make the béchamel sauce. Melt the butter in a heavy-based saucepan. Stir in the flour and cook gently for 1 minute, stirring to make a smooth paste. Remove the pan from the heat and gradually add the milk, beating well with a wooden spoon. If the mixture becomes lumpy, beat it briefly with a balloon whisk. Stir in all but 3 tablespoons of the Parmesan. Add a little nutmeg and salt and pepper and return the pan to the heat. Cook gently, stirring well, until the sauce is smooth and thickened.

Lower the fresh pasta sheets, if used, into the boiling water and return to the boil. Cook for 2 minutes and drain.

Spread a quarter of the meat sauce in a thin layer in a shallow, 1.5 litre (2½ pint) ovenproof dish. Spoon over a quarter of the béchamel sauce and spread the sauce over the meat with the back of a spoon. Arrange one-third of the pasta sheets over the sauce, trimming them to fit around the edges.

Repeat the layering of meat sauce, béchamel sauce and pasta into the dish, finishing with a layer of béchamel sauce. Sprinkle with the remaining Parmesan and plenty of freshly grated nutmeg. Bake in a preheated oven, 180°C (350°F), Gas Mark 4, for 40–45 minutes until golden.

moroccan
chicken stew

PREP: 15 MINUTES
COOKING TIME: 1 HOUR
SERVES: 4

4 tablespoons olive oil

1 chicken, about 1.75 g (3½ lb),
    cut into 8 pieces

12 pearl onions, peeled

2 garlic cloves, crushed

1 teaspoon each ground cumin,
    ginger and turmeric

½ teaspoon ground cinnamon

475 ml (16 fl oz) chicken stock

100 g (3½ oz) Kalamata olives

1 preserved lemon, chopped

2 tablespoons chopped fresh
    coriander

salt and pepper

couscous, rice or pasta, to serve

This dish uses preserved lemons, a bitter condiment that is added to many Moroccan meat dishes. They are available in Middle Eastern grocery stores and some supermarkets.

Heat the oil in a flameproof casserole dish and brown the chicken on all sides. Remove the pieces with a slotted spoon and set aside. Add the onions, garlic and spices and sauté over a low heat for 10 minutes or until just golden.

Return the chicken to the dish, stir in the stock and bring to the boil. Cover and simmer gently for 30 minutes. Add the olives, preserved lemon and coriander and cook for a further 15–20 minutes or until the chicken is really tender. Taste and adjust the seasoning if necessary and serve with couscous, rice or pasta.

> ‘I love this recipe. There is an element of comfort food about it, partly because of my Arabic roots. For me, when life is hard some of the tastes we had as children feel right. It is also really easy to make and I'm usually asked to bring it to parties.’
> **Samia al Qadhi**, **Joint Chief Executive, Breast Cancer Care**

spicy

couscous ✻

PREP: 10 MINUTES
COOKING TIME: 1 MINUTE
SERVES: 4–6

50 g (2 oz) pine nuts
250 g (8 oz) couscous
6 tablespoons olive oil
1 teaspoon dried coriander
1 teaspoon ground cumin
1 teaspoon dried chillies
50 g (2 oz) sultanas
finely grated rind and juice of
    1 lemon
2 tablespoons fresh mint
2 tablespoons fresh coriander
salt and pepper

Dry-roast the pine nuts and set aside. Place the couscous in a bowl, add 400 ml (14 fl oz) boiling water and leave to stand for 5 minutes then fluff up with a fork.

Heat the oil in a nonstick frying pan and gently fry the ground coriander, cumin and chillies for 1 minute. Add the sultanas then remove the pan from heat.

Add the lemon rind and lemon juice, mint and fresh coriander and season to taste with salt and pepper.

Combine the warm couscous with all the other ingredients.

Rosemary
Conley's
green thai chicken curry

‘ I give this recipe in support of my friend, Gwen Cherry, who had breast cancer 20 years ago. She is now fighting fit and still helps me at my diet and fitness classes every week ... I hope this recipe will help readers to realize that eating low fat doesn't mean eating food with a low taste. Achieving a healthy weight and eating a diet low in fat have enormous benefits to our general health. ’

PREP: 20 MINUTES
COOKING TIME: 30 MINUTES
SERVES: 4

2 red onions, sliced

3 garlic cloves, chopped

4 boneless, skinless chicken
   breasts, cut into dice

1 tablespoon ground coriander

½ teaspoon ground turmeric

¼ teaspoon fenugreek seeds or
   ground fenugreek

1 small red chilli, chopped

seeds from 4 cardamom pods

4 kaffir lime leaves (optional)

300 ml (½ pint) chicken stock

300 ml (½ pint) reduced-fat
   coconut milk

2 tablespoons chopped basil

125 g (4 oz) shredded spinach

salt and pepper

rice, to serve

Heat a nonstick wok or large frying pan and dry-fry the onions and garlic until soft and lightly coloured.

Add the chicken and cook briefly, turning once, to seal the outside of the meat. Season to taste with salt and pepper. Add the spices and continue cooking for 2 minutes then add the chicken stock, coconut milk and basil.

Reduce the heat and simmer gently for 20 minutes, uncovered, as the sauce thickens. Stir in the chopped spinach and serve with boiled rice.

margarita pizza

PREP: 10 MINUTES
COOKING TIME: 30–40 MINUTES
SERVES: 4

4 ready-to-cook pizza bases
300 g (10 oz) mozzarella cheese,
    cut into cubes
2 tablespoons black olives, pitted
olive oil, for brushing and
    drizzling

Fresh tomato sauce
3 tablespoons olive oil
2 red onions, finely sliced
2 garlic cloves, crushed and
    chopped
2 x 400 g (13 oz) cans chopped
    tomatoes
1 teaspoon red wine vinegar
pinch of sugar
salt and pepper

Often the simplest things in life are the best, as proved by this irresistibly moreish pizza.

Make the tomato sauce. Heat the oil in a large saucepan, add the onions and garlic and fry for 3 minutes. Add the tomatoes, vinegar and sugar and season to taste with salt and pepper. Turn up the heat and simmer until the mixture has reduced by half to make a thick and rich tomato sauce.

Put the pizza bases on lightly oiled baking sheets and brush with olive oil. Spoon the tomato sauce on to the pizzas, spreading it to within 5 mm (¼ inch) of the edges. Sprinkle over the cheese and olives and drizzle over a little more oil.

Place the pizzas at the top of a preheated oven, 230°C (450°F), Gas Mark 8, and bake for about 20 minutes until bubbling and golden.

> ‘ This is a recipe my mother used to make for me when I was a child. When I was going through my treatment I found it good to concentrate on making it instead of thinking about my situation. ’
>
> **Jacky Merrison,** **Breast Cancer Care volunteer, diagnosed 1994**

potato and
onion bread ❀

PREP: 15 MINUTES
COOKING TIME: ABOUT 25 MINUTES
SERVES: 8

1 tablespoon olive oil

1 onion, finely chopped

250 g (8 oz) self-raising flour

1 teaspoon baking powder

½ teaspoon salt

½ teaspoon paprika

175 g (6 oz) floury potatoes, cooked

1 egg

125 ml (4 fl oz) semi-skimmed milk

25 g (1 oz) butter, melted

1 teaspoon sesame seeds (optional)

Heat the oil in a medium frying pan and cook the onion for 5 minutes or until softened.

Sift the flour, baking powder, salt and paprika into a large bowl. Grate the potatoes into the dry ingredients and stir in the onion.

Beat the egg with the milk, stir in the melted butter and add to the ingredients in the bowl. Mix to a soft dough (it should be quite wet). Turn the dough out on to a floured surface and shape it into a 20 cm (8 inch) round.

Transfer the loaf to a lightly oiled baking sheet and sprinkle with sesame seeds (if used). Mark the dough into 8 wedges and cook in a preheated oven, 220°C (425°F), Gas Mark 7, for about 25 minutes or until browned. The bread is cooked when it sounds hollow when tapped on the base. Serve warm.

Marguerite Patten's
Patten's
rich chocolate cake

" Together with four neighbours and two of my relations, I know what it is to have had to battle with breast cancer. Fortunately, none of the seven of us know what it is like to watch a daughter face the illness, as happened to my old school friend, Amanda, who lost her daughter Becs in her 30s. I implore you to buy this book in quantities (it makes a super gift!). Please take every opportunity to find out how you can help to save the lives of more women like Becs.

From Marguerite Patten's daughter
Judith Patten Gunton (Mastectomy, 1994)

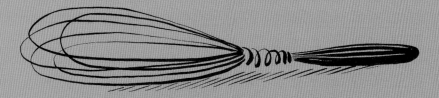

PREP: 30 MINUTES
COOKING TIME: 55–60 MINUTES
SERVES: 10

150 g (5 oz) best-quality plain
   chocolate
150 g (5 oz) butter
150 g (5 oz) icing sugar, sifted
5 large eggs, separated, and
   1 egg white
150 g (5 oz) self-raising flour,
   sifted
4 tablespoons apricot jam, sieved
225 ml (7½ fl oz) double cream,
   whipped
40 g (1½ oz) blanched flaked
   almonds, toasted

Line and grease the base and sides of a 23 cm (9 inch) round or a 20 cm (8 inch) square cake tin with baking parchment.

Break the chocolate into pieces and put them in a bowl with 1 tablespoon of water. Place over a saucepan of simmering water to melt, then leave to cool.

Cream together the butter and sugar and blend with the chocolate. Gradually beat the 5 egg yolks into the creamed mixture. Fold the flour into the other ingredients.

Whisk the 6 egg whites into soft peaks and beat a little into the cake mixture, then fold in the remainder. Spoon the mixture into the cake tin and bake in a preheated oven, 160°C (325°F), Gas Mark 3, for 55–60 minutes or until firm to the touch. Leave to cool in the tin for 5 minutes then turn out.

When the cake is cold, cut it in half horizontally and spread the lower piece with half the jam and some of the cream. Put the top on the cake and spread the remaining jam, then the cream over the top. Decorate with the almonds.

*P*hil Vickery's
carrot cake

'I love this cake – it's so moist and delicate. I normally coat mine in tempered bitter chocolate, but here I'm using icing, a twist on passion cake. The only sauce to serve with this is caramel apricot, a great foil to the rich sponge. The only thing you need to be careful of is to squeeze out the carrots very well, then weigh them after that. It's a bit of a labour getting all the bits together, but well worth it I can assure you!'

PREP: 40 MINUTES
COOKING TIME: 50–60 MINUTES
MAKES: 1 25 CM (10 INCH) CAKE

75 g (3 oz) Madeira cake crumbs
55 g (2¼ oz) plain flour, sieved
15 g (½ oz) baking powder
250 g (8 oz) chopped hazelnuts,
    skinned
300 g (10 oz) grated carrot, well
    squeezed out
1 tablespoon rum
5 eggs, separated
250 g (8 oz) caster sugar
2 large pinches of ground
    cinnamon
grated rind of 1 large lemon
1 teaspoon vanilla extract
4 tablespoons apricot jam, sieved
250 g (8 oz) white marzipan
400 g (13 oz) cream cheese
75 g (3 oz) icing sugar
grated rind of 1 orange, plus juice
    from ½ orange
Caramelized Apricot Sauce (see
    page 209), to serve

Grease and line a 25 cm (10 inch) loose-based cake tin that is 6 cm (2½ inches) deep. Mix together the cake crumbs, flour and baking powder, add the hazelnuts and carrot and mix well.

Whisk together the rum, egg yolks and half the caster sugar until thick and foamy. Fold in the cinnamon, lemon rind and vanilla extract.

Beat the egg whites until they break, add the remaining caster sugar and whisk until firm and glossy. Fold the crumb mixture into the egg yolk mixture, then finally fold-in the meringue.

Spoon the mixture into the prepared tin and bake in a preheated oven, 200°C (400°F), Gas Mark 6, for 30 minutes. Check to see if the cake has set, then reduce the heat to 160°C (325°F), Gas Mark 3, and cook for a further 20–30 minutes until the cake is nicely browned and firm to the touch. Remove from the oven and leave to cool in the tin for 10 minutes then remove to a wire rack to cool completely.

Spread the cake all over with apricot jam. Roll out the marzipan as thinly as possible, cover the cake and leave it to dry slightly.

Beat together the cream cheese, icing sugar and orange rind, and add the juice to loosen the mixture slightly. Spread it evenly over the cake, cut and serve with Caramelized Apricot Sauce.

papaya and
lime salad

PREP: 15 MINUTES PLUS COOLING
COOKING TIME: 5 MINUTES
SERVES: 4

3 firm, ripe papayas

2 whole limes, plus extra wedges
    to garnish

2 teaspoons light brown sugar

50 g (2 oz) blanched almonds,
    toasted

Papaya and lime complement each other beautifully. This simple but utterly delicious fruit salad can be served for brunch or as a light dessert.

Cut the papayas in half, scoop out the seeds and discard. Peel the halves, cut the flesh roughly into dice and put them in a bowl.

Finely grate the rind of both limes, then squeeze one of the limes and reserve the juice. Cut the pith off the second lime and segment the flesh over the bowl of diced papaya to catch the juice. Add the lime segments and grated rind to the papaya.

Pour the lime juice into a small pan with the sugar and heat gently until the sugar has dissolved. Remove from the heat and leave to cool. When the sweetened lime juice has cooled, pour it over the fruit and toss thoroughly. Add the toasted almonds to the salad and serve, garnished with lime wedges.

pink melon

delight

PREP: 5 MINUTES
NO COOK
SERVES: 2–3

150 g (5 oz) melon, cut into dice

150 g (5 oz) strawberries, plus
    extra to decorate

2–3 scoops orange sorbet

300 ml (½ pint) ginger ale

Host a girls night in and ask everyone to eat pink, drink pink and wear pink for **Breast Cancer Care**. The charity's In the Pink campaign encourages everyone to hold a pink event during October and it is a great way to catch up with friends and have fun while raising vital funds. You can cook up a feast using suggestions from this chapter and charge your friends an admission fee. For more girly-night-in ideas for next October's In the Pink campaign visit www.breastcancercare.org.uk.

Put the melon, strawberries and orange sorbet in a blender and blend at high speed for 15 seconds.

Gently stir in the ginger ale, pour into wine glasses and decorate each with a strawberry.

cranberry crush

PREP: 5 MINUTES
NO COOK
SERVES: 15

crushed ice
1.8 litres (3 pints) cranberry juice
600 ml (1 pint) orange juice
600 ml (1 pint) ginger ale
orange and lemon wedges, to
    decorate

Half-fill a large punch bowl with crushed ice. Pour in the cranberry and orange juices and stir to mix.

Top up with the ginger ale and decorate with orange and lemon wedges. Serve immediately.

cosmopolitan

PREP: 5 MINUTES
NO COOK
SERVES: 1

ice cubes
1½ measures citron vodka
1 measure Cointreau
1½ measures cranberry juice
¼ measure fresh lime juice
lime wheel, to decorate

Put the ice cubes in a cocktail shaker, add the citron vodka, Cointreau, cranberry juice and lime juice and shake well.

Strain into a chilled cocktail glass and add a lime wheel.

st clements

PREP: 5 MINUTES
NO COOK
SERVES: 1

4 ice cubes
2 measures fresh orange juice
2 measures bitter lemon
orange slice, to decorate

Put the ice cubes in a tumbler, pour in the orange juice and bitter lemon and stir together.

Serve decorated with the orange slice.

strawberry dawa

PREP: 5 MINUTES
NO COOK
SERVES: 1

3 strawberries
1 lime, sliced
dash of strawberry syrup
crushed ice
2 measures lemon vodka
split strawberry, to decorate

You can't go wrong with strawberries, especially when they're laced with vodka and lime.

Muddle the strawberries, lime and strawberry syrup in a rocks glass, fill it up with crushed ice, then add the vodka and stir well.

Serve with the muddling stick and decorate with a split strawberry.

world tour

Take a culinary tour around the world and a crash course in new flavours in this chapter that's packed full of delicious dishes from a diverse selection of countries. There's a chicken salad from Thailand, an unusual beef and aubergine curry from Malaysia and meatballs from Sweden, to name just a few.

Gregg Wallace's
chilli con carne

‘ This subject should be of great concern to everybody, and I'm delighted to help in this very small way. A blessing on the head to all those who are working so hard in this most necessary of causes ... I make absolutely no excuses for this recipe. It's a bloody good dish. I've loved it since I was a kid. ’

PREP: 15 MINUTES
COOKING TIME: 1 HOUR
20 MINUTES
SERVES: 4

500 g (1 lb) minced beef
1 tablespoon olive oil
1 large onion, chopped
1 teaspoon ground cumin
1 teaspoon ground coriander
2 teaspoons chilli powder
2 tablespoons tomato purée
4 fresh chillies, deseeded (if liked)
    and finely chopped
400 g (13 oz) can chopped
    tomatoes
410 g (13½ oz) can kidney beans,
    drained
1 teaspoon sugar
5 g (¼ oz) dark chocolate,
    chopped
salt and pepper

Heat a frying pan and dry-fry the beef until it is brown. Don't poke it. Remove the mince from the pan. Add the oil to the same pan and fry the onion for about 10 minutes or until it is softened and lightly browned. Return the mince to the pan.

Add the spices, tomato purée and chopped chillies and stir for a couple of minutes. Add the tomatoes, beans and sugar, and season to taste with salt and pepper.

Cover the pan and simmer for about 1 hour or until most of the liquid has evaporated and the mixture is quite dry, stirring occasionally.

Add the chocolate and simmer for another 5 minutes until it has completely melted.

orange
chicken curry ✿

PREP: 15 MINUTES
COOKING TIME: 30–35 MINUTES
SERVES: 4

25 g (1 oz) butter

1 onion, sliced

25 g (1 oz) plain flour

4–5 teaspoons hot curry powder

300 ml (½ pint) chicken stock

300 ml (½ pint) milk

1 medium chicken, roasted and
    meat removed

1 tablespoon tomato purée

1 teaspoon soft brown sugar

grated rind and juice of 1 small
    orange

handful of coriander, chopped
    (optional)

rice, to serve

Melt the butter in a large, heavy-based saucepan and sauté the onion until tender.

Mix together the flour and curry powder and add to the onion. Cook for a few minutes. Pour in the stock and milk. Gradually bring to the boil, stirring continuously, then add all the remaining ingredients except the coriander.

Mix well, cover and simmer for 20 minutes. Stir in the coriander, if using. Serve with rice.

❛ We tend to cook this in large quantities whenever we have friends round for lunch. It's loved by children and adults alike. I tend to regard it as my party atmosphere recipe – a large pot in the middle of the table with everyone tucking in! ❜
Dr Ann-Marie Todd,
touched by breast cancer

thai chicken

salad

PREP: 10 MINUTES
NO COOK
SERVES: 4

150 g (5 oz) cooked chicken
   breast, shredded
3 tablespoons coriander leaves
150 g (5 oz) pak choi, shredded

Dressing
1 tablespoon groundnut oil
1 tablespoon Thai fish sauce
juice of 1 lime
juice of 1 small orange
1 garlic clove, crushed
3 tablespoons roughly chopped
   basil leaves
30 g (1¼ oz) unsalted peanuts,
   skins removed and chopped
pepper

To garnish
2 spring onions, green stems
   only, shredded lengthways
1 plump red chilli, deseeded and
   sliced diagonally

While this chapter will take your tastebuds on a tantalizing world tour, why not engage your other senses and take a trek abroad in aid of **Breast Cancer Care**? The charity offers an exciting range of challenges including some of the most desirable and 'must see' destinations in the world including the Great Wall of China. You can experience new cultures, see some spectacular scenery, make new, lasting friendships and raise vital funds for Breast Cancer Care. For all the latest trekking destinations and information visit www.breastcancercare.org.uk

Make the dressing by shaking all the ingredients together in a screw-top jar.

Mix the chicken with the coriander leaves and stir in the dressing.

Line a serving dish with the pak choi, spoon the dressed chicken on top and serve chilled, garnished with spring onion shreds and red chilli slices.

malaysian beef and
aubergine curry

PREP: 20 MINUTES
COOKING TIME: ABOUT 1¾ HOURS
SERVES: 4–5

2 teaspoons cumin seeds

2 teaspoons coriander seeds

1 cinnamon stick

½ teaspoon crushed dried chillies

6 cloves

300 g (10 oz) aubergines

1 kg (2 lb) lean braising beef

5 tablespoons vegetable oil

2 large onions, sliced

1 tablespoon tamarind paste

2 tablespoons dark muscovado
    sugar

150 ml (¼ pint) coconut cream

salt

Put the cumin, coriander, cinnamon, dried chillies and cloves in a small food processor or a completely clean coffee grinder and grind as finely as possible.

Cut the aubergines into 2 cm (¾ inch) cubes. Discard any excess fat from the beef and cut the meat into chunks.

Heat the oil in a large, heavy-based frying pan and fry the onions for 6–8 minutes or until lightly browned. Add the blended spices and fry, stirring, for 1 minute. Add the beef and fry, stirring, for 2–3 minutes until the meat is coated in the spices.

Add 400 ml (14 fl oz) water, the tamarind paste and sugar and bring just to the boil. Cover with a lid and cook over the lowest heat for 1 hour or until the meat is tender.

Stir in the coconut cream and aubergines, cover the pan again and cook for a further 20–30 minutes until the aubergines are soft. Check the seasoning and serve.

" I cooked this recipe for my mother the very first time I entertained her and my father in my own home on Christmas Eve. She loved it and since her death from breast cancer I often look back to the happy memory of that special meal we shared together. "

Marion Pattison, mother diagnosed 1989

chinese
spare ribs ✳

PREP: 10 MINUTES, PLUS
MARINATING
COOKING TIME: 40–60 MINUTES
SERVES: 4

1 kg (2 lb) spare ribs

Marinade
3 tablespoons soy sauce
1 tablepoon honey
2 tablepoons hoisin sauce
1 tablepoon white vinegar
1 tablepoon sherry
1 garlic clove, finely chopped
1 teaspoon sugar
2 tablepoons stock

Make the marinade by blending all the marinade ingredients together in a large bowl.

Put the spare ribs in a non-metallic dish and pour over the marinade, turning the ribs to coat. Leave for at least 3 hours at room temperature or 5 hours in the refrigerator, turning and basting from time to time.

Transfer the spare ribs to a roasting tin, pour over the remaining marinade and roast in a preheated oven, 190°C (375°F), Gas Mark 5, for 30–45 minutes. Increase the oven temperature to 230°C (450°F), Gas Mark 8, and roast for a further 15 minutes (or grill for 10–15 minutes).

swedish
meatballs

PREP: 20 MINUTES
COOKING TIME: ABOUT
30 MINUTES
SERVES: 4

300 g (10 oz) lean veal mince

200 g (7 oz) lean pork mince

1 small onion, chopped

1 garlic clove, crushed

25 g (1 oz) breadcrumbs

1 egg yolk

3 tablespoons chopped flat leaf
    parsley

2 tablespoons vegetable oil

salt and pepper

Cranberry glaze

150 g (5 oz) good-quality
    cranberry sauce

100 ml (3½ fl oz) chicken or
    vegetable stock

2 tablespoons sweet chilli sauce

1 tablespoon lemon juice

Coated in a sweet, spicy cranberry glaze, these bite-sized meatballs make a good family supper dish with pappardelle or tagliatelle. Mixing the meat and flavourings in a food processor gives the meatballs their characteristic smooth texture.

Make the cranberry glaze. Combine the cranberry sauce, stock, chilli sauce and lemon juice in a small pan and heat gently until smooth. Leave to simmer gently for 5 minutes.

Put the veal and pork mince in a food processor with the onion, garlic, breadcrumbs, egg yolk, parsley and a little salt and pepper and blend until the mixture forms a fairly smooth paste that clings together.

Scoop teaspoonfuls of the paste and roll them into small balls between the palms of your hands.

Heat the oil in a large, heavy-based frying pan and fry half the meatballs for 8–10 minutes until golden. Drain and fry the remainder. Return all the meatballs to the pan and add the cranberry glaze. Cook gently for 2–3 minutes until very hot. Serve immediately.

new york-style
hot dogs

PREP: 25–30 MINUTES, PLUS PROVING
COOKING TIME: 10–12 MINUTES
MAKES: 20 HOT DOGS

20 mini cocktail frankfurters or
    sausages
American-style mustard
tomato ketchup

Hot dog buns
250 g (8 oz) strong white flour,
    sifted
pinch of salt
2 teaspoons olive oil
1 heaped teaspoon easy-blend
    dried yeast
beaten egg, for brushing

The hot dog stand is a quintessential New York institution and one that has been feeding hungry passers-by since the late 1800s.

Make the buns. Put the flour in a bowl with the salt, make a well in the centre and add 165 ml (5½ fl oz) hand-warm water and oil. Sprinkle the dried yeast over the liquid and leave for 2–3 minutes to dissolve. Gently draw in the flour from the sides of the bowl and knead to a sticky dough. Turn the dough out on to a floured surface and knead for 10 minutes until elastic and smooth. Place in a bowl, cover with clingfilm and leave to rise in a warm place for 1½ hours.

Lightly flour a baking sheet. Knock back the dough, divide it into 20 portions and shape each one into a cylinder, about 3 cm (1¼ inches) long. Put the rolls on the baking sheet, cover and leave to rise for 20 minutes.

Brush each roll with beaten egg and place in a preheated oven, 200°C (400°F), Gas Mark 6, for 10–12 minutes or until lightly browned and cooked through. Remove from the oven and cool on a wire rack.

Split each roll lengthways along the top. Fill with a cocktail frankfurter or sausage. Pipe over the mustard and ketchup and serve.

nut koftas

with minted yogurt

PREP: 20 MINUTES
COOKING TIME: 10 MINUTES
SERVES: 4

4 tablespoons vegetable oil
1 onion, chopped
½ teaspoon chilli flakes
2 garlic cloves, chopped
1 tablespoon curry paste
425 g (14 oz) can cannellini
    beans, rinsed and drained
125 g (4 oz) ground almonds
75 g (3 oz) chopped almonds
1 small egg
plain flour, for dusting
salt and pepper
8 wooden skewers

Minted yogurt
200 ml (7 fl oz) Greek yogurt
2 tablespoons chopped mint

Lemon dressing
2 tablespoons vegetable oil
1 tablespoon lemon juice

Heat 3 tablespoons oil in a frying pan, add the onion and fry for 4 minutes. Add the chilli flakes, garlic and curry paste and fry for another minute.

Pour the mixture into a blender or food processor with the beans, ground and chopped almonds, egg and a little salt and pepper and blend until the mixture starts to stick together.

Put a little flour on your hands, take about one-eighth of the mixture and mould it around a skewer, forming it into a sausage about 2.5 cm (1 inch) thick. Make 7 more koftas in the same way.

Brush the koftas with the remaining oil. Cook under a moderate grill for about 5 minutes until golden, turning once.

Meanwhile, make the minted yogurt. Mix together the yogurt and mint in a small bowl. In a separate bowl, make the lemon dressing by mixing together the oil with the lemon juice and a little salt and pepper.

Brush the koftas with the lemon dressing, dollop on the minted yogurt and serve.

Julia Bradbury's
keftaides

PREP: 25 MINUTES, PLUS
MARINATING
COOKING TIME: 6 MINUTES PER
BATCH
SERVES: 4

2 slices of bread

150 ml (¼ pint) red wine

500 g (1 lb) minced beef or lamb

1 large onion, finely chopped

5 garlic cloves, finely chopped

4 tablespoons finely chopped
  mint

50 g (2 oz) finely grated Parmesan
  cheese

2 eggs, beaten

flour, for coating

salt and pepper

3 tablespoons olive oil

Pronounced 'keftethes', these Greek meatballs are delicious and easy to make. Serve them with a green salad with feta cheese and black olives.

Soak the bread in the red wine for 2–3 minutes. Mix the meat, onion and garlic. Add the soaked bread, mint and cheese. Season to taste with salt and pepper and add the eggs.

Mix everything together and leave to stand in the refrigerator for as long as possible, or preferably overnight.

Form the mixture into meatballs about 3.5 cm (1½ inches) across. Coat in flour and fry in hot oil for 5–6 minutes, turning occasionally until browned (make sure the centre of the meatball is cooked). Drain on kitchen paper to absorb the excess oil and serve immediately.

chicken
parmigiana

PREP: 25 MINUTES
COOKING TIME: ABOUT 1¼ HOURS
SERVES: 4

8 tablespoons olive oil

1 onion, finely chopped

3 garlic cloves, crushed

400 g (13 oz) can chopped
    tomatoes

100 g (3½ oz) tomato paste

2 teaspoons caster sugar

25 g (1 oz) basil, torn into small
    pieces

500 g (1 lb) aubergines

4 chicken breasts fillets, skinned

125 g (4 oz) Parmesan cheese,
    freshly grated

salt and pepper

Heat 2 tablespoons oil in a heavy-based saucepan and fry the onion and garlic for 3 minutes. Add the tomatoes, tomato paste, sugar and salt and pepper to taste and bring to the boil. Reduce the heat slightly and cook, uncovered, until the sauce is rich and pulpy. Add half the torn basil.

Cut the aubergines across into slices 5 mm (¼ inch) thick and place them on a foil-lined grill rack. Brush with a little oil and grill until golden. Turn the slices, brush with more oil and grill again until they are golden.

Thinly slice the chicken breasts and fry the meat in the remaining oil until it is cooked through, which will take about 8 minutes.

Place one-third of the aubergines in a shallow, 1.8 litre (3 pint) ovenproof dish and cover with one-third of the chicken, sauce, basil and cheese. Repeat the layering, finishing with sauce and cheese.

Bake in a preheated oven, 180°C (350°F), Gas Mark 4, for 40 minutes until the cheese is melted and a pale golden colour.

> ' I am known to make a mean quiche and always keep a spare one in the freezer for emergencies. '
>
> **Kim Smith,** diagnosed 2000

quiche ✳

PREP: 40 MINUTES PLUS CHILLING
COOKING TIME: ABOUT
55 MINUTES
SERVES: 6

1 tablespoon oil
1 small onion, chopped
175 g (6 oz) mushrooms, sliced
8 slices unsmoked back bacon
3 large eggs
300 ml (½ pint) milk
good dash Worcestershire Sauce
2 tablespoons Italian seasoning
125 g (4 oz) Cheddar cheese, grated
1 large tomato, sliced
dried oregano, to sprinkle
salt and pepper

Pastry
125 g (4 oz) plain flour
125 g (4 oz) self-raising flour
125 g (4 oz) butter
about 6 tablespoons cold water

Make the pastry. Sift the flours together in a bowl. Dice the butter and rub into the flour to resemble breadcrumbs. Make a well in the centre, add enough cold water to mix into a firm dough. Cover and chill in the refrigerator for 30 minutes.

Roll out the pastry on a lightly floured surface and use it to line a greased 25 cm (10 inch) flan tin. Bake blind in a preheated oven, 180°C (350°F), Gas Mark 4, for 15 minutes.

Meanwhile, heat the oil in a frying pan and gently fry the onion, mushrooms and chopped bacon for 10 minutes. Allow to cool. Put the eggs, milk and seasonings in a bowl and beat together.

Fill the flan case with the onion mixture then top with the cheese. Pour over the egg mixture. Arrange the tomato slices on top and sprinkle over the oregano.

Cook in the oven for 40 minutes or until the top is golden-brown.

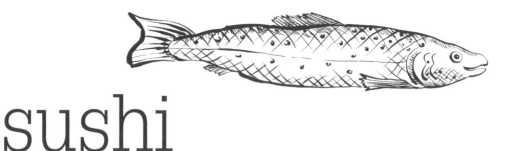

sushi

PREP: 30 MINUTES, PLUS COOLING
COOKING TIME: 15 MINUTES
SERVES: 4–6

225 g (7½ oz) Japanese sushi rice
4 spring onions, very finely
    shredded
4 tablespoons seasoned rice
    vinegar
1 tablespoon caster sugar
25 g (1 oz) pickled ginger,
    shredded
1 tablespoon toasted sesame
    seeds
100 g (3½ oz) wild salmon
1 large sole fillet
3–4 sheets of nori
10 cooked peeled prawns
light soy sauce, to serve

This simplified version of rolled sushi is similar in flavour but takes half the time to make. You can use any mixture of fish as long as you can be sure that it's absolutely fresh.

Put the rice in a large, heavy-based saucepan with 450 ml (¾ pint) water. Bring slowly to the boil, then reduce the heat and simmer, half-covered with a lid, for 5–8 minutes or until all the water is absorbed. Cover completely and cook gently for 5 minutes or until the rice is tender and sticky. Turn into a bowl and leave to cool.

Stir the spring onions, vinegar, sugar, ginger and sesame seeds into the rice. Slice the salmon and sole into small strips.

Use scissors to cut the nori sheets into 6 cm (2½ inch) squares. Dampen your hands and mould the rice into little ovals. Arrange the rice ovals diagonally over the nori squares.

Bring the pointed ends on opposite sides of the nori over the rice and arrange a piece of fish or a prawn on top. Arrange on a serving platter and serve with a small bowl of soy sauce for dipping.

Mitchell Tonks'
asian fishcakes

PREP: 25 MINUTES
COOKING TIME: 15 MINUTES
SERVES: 4

1 lemon grass stalk

1 teaspoon Thai fish sauce

2–3 kaffir lime leaves

1 teaspoon fresh root ginger,
    peeled and grated

1 garlic clove

½ red chilli, not too hot

juice of 1 lime

1 tablespoon chopped coriander

400 g (13 oz) white fish fillet, such
    as cod, haddock, pollock or
    gurnard

6 tablespoons mashed potato

flour, for dusting

2 tablespoons olive oil

sweet chilli jam, to serve

Put the lemon grass, fish sauce, lime leaves, ginger, garlic, chilli, lime juice and coriander in a blender and blitz to make a smooth paste. Poach the fish in water for 10 minutes. Drain well and allow to cool, then flake.

Mix a few tablespoons of the paste into some mashed potato and the fish. Divide the mixture into 8 equal portions and roughly shape into fishcakes on a floured surface. Heat the oil and fry for 2–3 minutes on each side until golden. Serve hot with sweet chilli jam.

" A tasty fishcake, great for any time of the year. Fish works really well with these tangy fresh spices. Serve with some sweet chilli jam, homemade is really the best. "

moussaka

PREP: 25 MINUTES
COOKING TIME: 1½ HOURS
SERVES: 4

500 g (1 lb) aubergines
8 tablespoons olive oil
1 large onion, finely chopped
500 g (1 lb) lean minced lamb
400 g (13 oz) can chopped
    tomatoes
1 teaspoon dried oregano
4 garlic cloves, crushed
150 ml (¼ pint) red wine
300 g (10 oz) Greek-style yogurt
2 eggs, beaten
100 g (3½ oz) feta cheese,
    crumbled
salt and pepper

Brushing the aubergines with oil and grilling rather than frying them gives a lighter, less 'fatty-tasting' dish. The tangy feta topping is also lovely and light, but you can use a more substantial cheese, such as Gruyère or Cheddar, if you prefer.

Cut the aubergines into thin slices and arrange them in a single layer on a foil-lined grill rack. Blend 5 tablespoons oil with plenty of salt and pepper and brush a little over the aubergines. Grill until golden, then turn and grill again, brushing with more oil. (If necessary, grill in 2 batches.)

Heat the remaining oil in a large, heavy-based saucepan and fry the onion and lamb for 10 minutes until browned. Stir in the tomatoes, oregano, garlic, wine and a little salt and pepper. Cover and cook gently for 20 minutes or until pulpy.

Spread a quarter of the meat sauce in the base of a shallow, 2 litre (3½ pint) ovenproof dish and cover with one-third of the aubergine slices. Repeat the layering, finishing with the meat sauce.

Beat together the yogurt and eggs and spoon over the meat. Crumble over the feta and bake in a preheated oven, 180°C (350°F), Gas Mark 4, for about 45 minutes until the topping is golden.

spicy spanish
chicken stew ✳

PREP: 25 MINUTES
COOKING TIME: 1¾ HOURS
SERVES: 4–6

3 tablespoons olive oil

1 large onion, chopped

1 celery stick, chopped

2 carrots, chopped

150 g (5 oz) mushrooms, sliced

4 chicken breasts, skinned and
    cut into large chunks

2 x 400 g (13 oz) cans chopped
    tomatoes

1 chicken stock cube, crumbled

150 ml (¼ pint) glass of red or
    white wine (optional)

12 cm (5 inches) chorizo sausage

1½ tablespoons clear honey

1 small chilli, chopped or
    ½ teaspoon chilli powder

2 garlic cloves, chopped

1½ teaspoons salt

pepper to taste

410 g (13½ oz) can kidney beans

2 teaspoons cornflour (optional)

Heat the oil in a large, heavy-based saucepan over a moderate heat, add the onion, celery, carrots and mushrooms and fry gently for about 3 minutes.

Increase the heat, add the chicken and cook until it is browned. Reduce the heat and add the tomatoes, stock cube, wine (if used), chorizo, honey, chilli, garlic and season with salt and pepper.

Cook for a further 1½ hours until the chicken is thoroughly cooked and the sauce is thick.

Add the beans and cook for a further 10 minutes. If the sauce needs thickening, mix the cornflour with a little water and stir the paste into the sauce.

❝ I found that this was an easy meal for either myself or my husband to cook at those times when we just didn't feel like cooking. For those like myself who had heartburn during chemo, the chilli can be omitted. ❞
Irene Mackay, diagnosed 2006

Anjum Nida Rahman's
yogurt chicken

' This is a delicious dish whose simplicity belies its full flavour. This dish has been in my family for as long back as I can remember and has always been a family favourite. It is easy to make and can be made with the minimum of spices and even less effort. As a bonus there is very little oil used in the dish, which relies on quality chicken and good-quality, fresh yogurt for its depth of flavour and creaminess. I recommend cooking this dish for anyone: the girls coming over for a night in, the boys on football night or just for a simple family meal, without the chillies, of course. I serve this dish with some green vegetables and rösti, but you can do some sautéed potatoes and peas for a simple meal. '

PREP: 15 MINUTES, PLUS
MARINATING
COOKING TIME: 35 MINUTES
SERVES: 4

1 chicken, about 1.3 kg (2½ lb),
   skinned and jointed into equal
   pieces so that the breast is
   cut in half (your butcher will
   do this)
2 tablespoons vegetable oil
1–2 green chillies, cut open
   (optional)
1 small onion, chopped
2 small or 1 large black
   cardamom pods
handful of finely chopped fresh
   coriander stalks and leaves
salt and pepper

Marinade
40 g (1¼ oz) garlic (about 7 fat
   cloves), peeled
20 g (¾ oz) fresh root ginger,
   peeled
400 g (13 oz) yogurt
4 teaspoons ground coriander
½–1 teaspoon red chilli powder
1 teaspoon garam masala
1½ teaspoons salt or to taste
½ teaspoon ground cumin

Cut some slashes in the chicken flesh at 1 cm (½ inch) intervals or prick it all over. Put the chicken in a non-metallic dish.

Make the marinade. Purée the garlic and ginger with some of the yogurt to make a smooth paste and stir in the remaining marinade ingredients. Add to the chicken and leave to marinate in the refrigerator for as long as possible, preferably overnight. Bring back to room temperature before you start to cook.

Heat the oil in a frying pan and fry the chillies and the onion for about 6 minutes or until they are soft. Add the chicken with the cardamom pods and continue cooking over a high heat for 15–20 minutes until the sauce becomes creamy and covers only one-third of the chicken.

Cover the saucepan and cook the chicken, over a low heat, for a further 10–15 minutes, stirring occasionally, until the meat is tender and the sauce is rich and creamy. While it cooks, check that there is sufficient water in the pan and add a splash if necessary. Stir in the coriander, check the seasoning and serve.

linzertorte

PREP: 25 MINUTES
COOKING TIME: 25–30 MINUTES
SERVES: 6

150 g (6 oz) plain flour

½ teaspoon ground cinnamon

75 g (3 oz) butter, diced

50 g (2 oz) sugar

50 g (2 oz) ground almonds

2 teaspoons finely grated
   lemon rind

2 large egg yolks

about 1 tablespoon lemon juice

325 g (11 oz) raspberry jam

icing sugar, to decorate

This delicious tart takes its name from the Austrian town of Linz. It is distinguished by the pastry, which is made with ground almonds.

Sift the flour and cinnamon into a bowl. Rub in the butter until the mixture resembles fine breadcrumbs. Add the sugar, ground almonds and lemon rind. Bind the dough with the egg yolks and enough lemon juice to make a stiff dough. Turn out the dough on to a floured surface and knead lightly.

Roll out two-thirds of the dough and line a greased 18–20 cm (7–8 inch) fluted flan ring placed on a baking sheet. Make sure the dough is evenly rolled out, press it to the shape of the ring and trim off the excess.

Fill the tart with the raspberry jam. Roll out the reserved dough and the trimmings and cut them into long strips with a pastry wheel or knife. Use these to make a lattice over the jam.

Bake the tart in a preheated oven, 190°C (375°F) Gas Mark 5, for 25–30 minutes until golden-brown. Leave to cool, then remove the flan ring. Sprinkle icing sugar over the top of the tart just before serving.

apple and cranberry
streusel

PREP: 20 MINUTES
COOKING TIME: 50–60 MINUTES
SERVES: 6–8

250 g (8 oz) self-raising flour
175 g (6 oz) unsalted butter, diced
175 g (6 oz) golden caster sugar,
   plus 2 tablespoons
1 egg
4 tart dessert apples, such as
   Granny Smith
50 g (2 oz) dried cranberries
icing sugar, for dusting

There's only a tenuous link between this cake and a traditional German streusel, but it is easy to make and delicious served slightly warm with a dollop of cream.

Grease an 18 cm (7 inch) round springform tin or loose-based cake tin. Put the flour in a food processor and add the butter. Blend until the mixture resembles fine breadcrumbs. Add 175 g (6 oz) sugar and blend until the mixture just starts to make a coarse crumble.

Spoon out 175 g (6 oz) of the mixture and add the egg to the remainder in the food processor. Blend to a firm paste. Turn the paste into the base of the tin, pressing it down gently in an even layer.

Peel, core and slice the apples. Toss them in a bowl with the cranberries and the remaining caster sugar. Scatter the fruit into the tin and sprinkle with the reserved crumble mix.

Bake the streusel in a preheated oven, 180°C (350°F), Gas Mark 4, for 50–60 minutes or until deep golden. Leave to cool in the tin and serve lightly dusted with icing sugar.

white chocolate
biscotti

PREP: 15 MINUTES, PLUS COOLING
COOKING TIME: 35 MINUTES
MAKES: 24 BISCUITS

300 g (10 oz) white chocolate
25 g (1 oz) unsalted butter,
    softened
225 g (7½ oz) self-raising flour
50 g (2 oz) light muscovado sugar
2 eggs
1 teaspoon vanilla extract
100 g (3½ oz) pecan nuts, roughly
    chopped
icing sugar, to dust

These gorgeous biscuits are baked in one piece, then sliced and baked again to crisp them up. Serve them the Italian way, dunked into dessert wine or with some creamy hot chocolate.

Chop 100 g (3½ oz) of the chocolate into small pieces. Break up the remainder and melt it in a small bowl with the butter. Leave to cool. Sift the flour into a mixing bowl and stir in the sugar, eggs, vanilla extract, nuts and melted chocolate mixture.

Add the chopped chocolate and mix to a dough. Tip the mixture on to a lightly floured surface and halve the dough.

Shape each half into a log about 25 cm (10 inches) long and flatten to a depth of 2 cm (¾ inch). Space well apart on a large, lightly greased baking sheet and bake in a preheated oven, 190°C (375°F), Gas Mark 5, for 18–20 minutes until risen, golden and firm. Remove from the oven and reduce the oven temperature to 160°C (325°F), Gas Mark 3.

Leave the biscuit logs to cool for 20 minutes, then use a serrated knife to cut each length into slices 2 cm (¾ inch) thick. Space them slightly apart on the baking sheet and bake for a further 15 minutes. Dust with icing sugar and transfer to a wire rack to cool.

tarte tatin

PREP: 20 MINUTES, PLUS CHILLING
COOKING TIME: 35–40 MINUTES
SERVES: 4–6

50 g (2 oz) butter

50 g (2 oz) caster sugar

6 dessert apples, peeled, cored
and quartered

175 g (6 oz) pâte sucrée

double cream or crème fraîche,
to serve

This version of the classic French tart is deceptively simple to make. Use well-flavoured, crunchy apples, such as Cox's, and unsalted butter.

Melt the butter and sugar in a 20 cm (8 inch) ovenproof frying pan. When the mixture is golden-brown, add the apples and toss them in the syrup to coat them. Cook for a few minutes until the apples start to caramelize.

Roll out the pastry on a lightly floured surface to a round, a little larger than the pan. Put it over the apples, tucking the edges of the pastry inside the edge of the pan until it fits neatly.

Bake in a preheated oven, 200°C (400°F), Gas Mark 6, for 35–40 minutes until the pastry is golden. Leave to cool in the pan for 5 minutes, then put a large plate on top of the pan and invert the tart on to it. Serve warm with cream or crème fraîche.

a little romance

Why not treat that special someone to one of these delicious dishes? We've gathered together a range of recipes that are bound to get cupid's arrow quivering. For something quick and easy try *Fillet Steak with Mustard Sauce* followed by *Love Hearts.* Or if you're feeling adventurous, go for the *Quail with Lime, Chilli and Ginger.*

*J*amie Oliver's
japanese-style
tuna carpaccio

' This is a wonderfully simple, almost exotic light meal that fills you with a big smile. It's food for lovers! For the tuna, try to get bluefin or bigeye, but yellowfin can be really good as well. Your tuna needs to be red and almost waxy-looking, and should smell of nothing but the sea. '

PREP: 15 MINUTES
NO COOK
SERVES: 2

200 g (7 oz) piece fresh tuna

1 small fresh red chilli, deseeded

small piece of mooli (white Asian radish) or a handful of radishes

purple shiso leaves or fresh coriander sprigs (optional)

1 lime, halved

2 teaspoons soy sauce

2 tablespoons extra virgin olive oil, to drizzle

Shiso is a Japanese herb with a strong flavour reminiscent of aniseed. A brilliant Japanese trick is to stuff the chilli inside the mooli. This means that when you grate it you get a pink-coloured, chilli-flavoured radish pulp, which is fantastic. You can get the same effect by finely chopping the chilli and grating normal radishes.

Get your tuna, and with a long sharp knife slice it as thinly as you can. Once you've sliced it, you can smooth it over with the side of your knife to make it even thinner. Divide this in one layer between your plates, or it's even nicer to serve it on one big plate.

Next, cut a V-shaped vertical slit in the mooli and stuff the chilli in before grating it. If you're using radishes instead, then grate them, finely chop the chillies and mix together. Blob it and its juice over the tuna slices and sprinkle over the shiso or fresh coriander.

When you serve it to your loved one at the table, all you need to do is squeeze half a lime equally over the fish and finish with the soy sauce and a drizzle of olive oil.

smoked salmon and
dill soufflé

PREP: 30 MINUTES
COOKING TIME: 35–40 MINUTES
SERVES: 4

65 g (2½ oz) butter

3 tablespoons fresh breadcrumbs

50 g (2 oz) plain flour

300 ml (½ pint) milk

4 tablespoons full-fat crème
    fraîche

3 tablespoons chopped dill

grated rind of 1 lemon

4 eggs, separated

100 g (3½ oz) sliced smoked
    salmon, cut into thin strips

salt and pepper

To serve

slices of smoked salmon
    (optional)

lemon wedges

Lightly grease a soufflé dish, 15 cm (6 inches) across by 9 cm (3¾ inches) deep, with a little butter, then line the dish with the breadcrumbs. Attach a soufflé collar that stands 8 cm (3 inches) higher than the dish.

Melt the remaining butter in a heavy-based saucepan, stir in the flour and cook for 1 minute. Gradually mix in the milk and bring to the boil, stirring until thickened and smooth.

Remove the pan from the heat and stir in the crème fraîche, dill, lemon rind and egg yolks. Season to taste with salt and pepper. Cover and leave to cool.

Whisk the egg whites into stiff, moist-looking peaks. Fold the strips of smoked salmon into the cooled sauce, then add a large spoonful of egg whites to loosen the mixture. Gently fold in the remaining egg whites.

Pour the mixture into the prepared soufflé dish so that it is three-quarters full. Bake in a preheated oven, 190°C (375°F), Gas Mark 5, for 30–35 minutes until the soufflé is well risen, the top is browned and there is a slight wobble to the centre.

Quickly snip the string off the soufflé collar and gently peel away the paper. Spoon the soufflé on to plates. Serve with extra slices of smoked salmon, if liked, and lemon wedges.

skate wings

with caper and olive sauce

PREP: 10 MINUTES
COOKING TIME: ABOUT
10 MINUTES
SERVES: 4

4 tablespoons extra virgin
olive oil

4 skate wings, about 250 g (8 oz)
each, trimmed

4 tablespoons flour, seasoned
with salt and pepper

herb and baby leaf salad, to serve

Caper and olive butter

100 g (3½ oz) butter

1 garlic clove, chopped

2 tablespoons capers in brine,
drained

50 g (2 oz) pitted black olives

juice of 1 lemon

1 tablespoon chopped curly
parsley

1 tablespoon chopped chervil

salt and pepper

This unusual butter, which is flavoured with capers and black olives combined with lemon juice, garlic and herbs, makes a lively accompaniment to pan-fried skate. It is essential that this dish is prepared quickly and served immediately.

Heat the oil in a large frying pan over a moderately high heat. Sprinkle the skate wings with a little seasoned flour and place them in the pan. (You may need to do this in 2 batches.) Fry the skate for 2–3 minutes on each side until cooked through then transfer them to hot serving plates.

Make the caper and olive butter. Wipe the pan with kitchen paper and return it to the heat. Melt the butter and when the froth has died down add the garlic and bubble gently until it turns golden-brown. Tip in the capers, olives, lemon juice, parsley and chervil and stir quickly for 20 seconds. Season with salt and pepper and pour a little of the butter over each skate wing. Serve immediately with a herb and baby leaf salad.

fillet steak

with mustard sauce

PREP: 8 MINUTES
COOKING TIME: 14–16 MINUTES
SERVES: 4

50 g (2 oz) butter

4 shallots, finely chopped

1 tablespoon wholegrain mustard

1 teaspoon Dijon mustard

2 tablespoons black olive
    tapenade paste

150 ml (¼ pint) cider

4 thick fillet steaks, about 200 g
    (7 oz) each, at room
    temperature

2 tablespoons coarsely ground
    black peppercorns

2 tablespoons extra virgin olive
    oil

2 tablespoons Calvados or
    brandy

2 tablespoons crème fraîche

2 tablespoons chopped tarragon

salt and pepper

Heat the butter in a frying pan until it has melted and is beginning to froth. Add the shallots and fry gently for 5–6 minutes or until softened. Add the wholegrain and Dijon mustards and tapenade and pour in the cider. Simmer gently for 2 minutes then remove from the heat.

Press the steaks into the peppercorns. Heat the oil in a large frying pan and cook the steaks for 1–2 minutes on each side or longer if you like your meat well done. Pour over the Calvados or brandy and carefully set it alight with a long taper.

Arrange the steaks on warm serving plates while you quickly scrape the Calvados and meat juices into the cider sauce. Stir in the crème fraîche and tarragon, season to taste with salt and pepper and gently warm the sauce without letting it boil. Pour a little sauce over each fillet steak and serve immediately with steamed asparagus, homemade chips and a dish of mustardy mayonnaise.

lamb cutlets

with anchovies, rosemary and lemon

PREP: 15 MINUTES, PLUS
MARINATING
COOKING TIME: 15 MINUTES
SERVES: 4

finely grated rind and juice
    of ½ lemon
2 garlic cloves, crushed
2 tablespoons extra virgin olive
    oil, plus extra for brushing
4 rosemary sprigs, finely chopped
4 anchovy fillets in oil, drained
    and finely chopped
2 tablespoons lemon cordial
12 lamb cutlets
4 sweet potatoes, baked in their
    skins
salt and pepper
rocket leaves, to serve

Put the lemon rind and juice in a bowl and add the garlic, oil, rosemary, anchovies and lemon cordial. Mix thoroughly and add the lamb cutlets. Season to taste with salt and pepper, turn the cutlets to coat and set aside for 15 minutes to marinate.

Cook the lamb cutlets under a preheated hot grill for 3–5 minutes on each side or until charred and cooked through. Keep warm and leave to rest while you prepare the sweet potato skins.

Cut the baked sweet potatoes into quarters, scoop out some of the flesh and brush the skins with oil. Season with salt and pepper and cook under the hot grill until crisp. Serve with the lamb cutlets and rocket leaves.

pork

with rosemary and fennel

PREP: 15 MINUTES
COOKING TIME: 30 MINUTES
SERVES: 2

750 g (1½ lb) pork fillet, trimmed
    of any fat
handful of rosemary sprigs,
    broken into small pieces
3 garlic cloves, sliced lengthways
4 tablespoons olive oil
2 fennel bulbs
300 ml (½ pint) white wine
150 g (5 oz) mascarpone cheese
salt and pepper

Pierce the pork with a sharp knife and insert small sprigs of rosemary and slices of garlic evenly all over the fillet. Heat 2 tablespoons oil in a frying pan, add the pork fillet and fry for 5 minutes or until browned.

Trim the fennel, cut it into wedges and remove the solid central core. Lightly oil a roasting tin, put the trimmed fennel in it and drizzle over the remaining olive oil. Place the pork on top and season. Place in a preheated oven, 230°C (450°F), Gas Mark 8, and roast for 25 minutes.

Add the wine to the frying pan in which the pork was fried and simmer until reduced by half. Add the mascarpone, season to taste with salt and pepper and stir to mix thoroughly.

Serve the pork in slices with the wedges of fennel. Pour the sauce into the roasting tin and simmer over a low heat on top of the stove until it has slightly thickened. Stir well and spoon over the pork and fennel.

bacon steaks
with pears and mustard sauce

PREP: 10 MINUTES
COOKING TIME: 20–25 MINUTES
SERVES: 4

2 ripe, juicy pears

4 bacon or gammon steaks

25 g (1 oz) butter, melted

150 g (5 oz) crème fraîche

2 tablespoons finely chopped
    curly parsley

2 teaspoons wholegrain mustard

pepper

Use ripe, juicy pears for a lovely contrast with the meat. If you bought the meat from a butcher and it was cut from a large joint soak it overnight before cooking to reduce the saltiness. Serve with a buttery celeriac mash.

Quarter the pears and arrange them in a roasting tin with the bacon steaks. Brush with the melted butter and season with black pepper. Bake in a preheated oven, 190°C (375°F), Gas Mark 5, for 20–25 minutes or until the bacon is cooked and the pears are soft and juicy.

Drain the meat and pears and transfer them to warm serving plates. Add the crème fraîche, parsley and mustard to the roasting tin.

Bring the sauce to the boil and let the mixture bubble for a couple of minutes until thickened. Pour it over the steaks and serve.

smoked chicken

and wild mushroom tart

PREP: 20 MINUTES, PLUS CHILLING
COOKING TIME: 55–60 MINUTES
SERVES: 6

375 g (12 oz) shortcrust pastry,
    thawed if frozen
1–2 tablespoons olive oil
125 g (4 oz) mixed wild
    mushrooms
½ cooked smoked chicken
100 g (3½ oz) sun-blushed
    tomatoes
100 g (3½ oz) Cheddar cheese,
    grated
3 eggs
300 ml (½ pint) double cream
2 tablespoons chopped tarragon

Roll out the pastry on a lightly floured surface and use it to line a 30 x 20 cm (12 x 8 inch) fluted tart tin. Chill the pastry case for 30 minutes, then bake blind in a preheated oven, 200°C (400°F), Gas Mark 6, for 15 minutes. Remove the paper and beans or foil and return to the oven for a further 5 minutes. Leave the oven on.

Heat the oil in a frying pan and cook the mushrooms for 3–4 minutes until they are lightly coloured and cooked.

Remove the chicken meat from the bones and carcass, cutting the larger pieces into bite-sized chunks. Sprinkle the chicken, tomatoes, mushrooms and Cheddar into the pastry case.

Mix together the eggs, cream and tarragon. Pour over the filling and bake in the oven for 30–35 minutes until golden and set.

> ' In 2005 I joined the few men in the UK to be treated for breast cancer. While going through the usual list of treatments I was unable to find the energy needed for my usual pastime, gardening, so I turned to my second love, cooking. '
>
> **Alan Hobson**, diagnosed 2005

light smoked
haddock bake ✽

PREP: 20 MINUTES
COOKING TIME: 1½–1¾ HOURS
SERVES: 4–5

15 g (½ oz) butter
500 g (1 lb) smoked haddock
2 onions, finely chopped
175 g (6 oz) frozen peas or
　　sweetcorn
700 g (1 lb 6 oz) potatoes, thinly
　　sliced
175 g (6 oz) Red Leicester
　　cheese, grated
300 ml (½ pint) double cream
pepper
green beans, to serve

Heat the butter in a frying pan and cook the haddock until it starts to flake. Put half the haddock in a shallow ovenproof dish and scatter half the onions over the fish.

Layer half the peas or sweetcorn over the onion and half the potatoes over the peas. Season to taste with pepper. Repeat the layers with the remaining fish, onion, peas and potatoes. Cover the top layer of potatoes with the cheese and pour the cream over the top.

Cook in a preheated oven, 190°C (375°F), Gas Mark 5, for 1¼–1½ hours or until the potatoes are cooked. If the cheese becomes too brown, cover it with foil. Serve with green beans.

quail with lime,

chilli and ginger

PREP: 15 MINUTES, PLUS
MARINATING
COOKING TIME: 20 MINUTES
SERVES: 2

This quick and easy dish is great for preparing several hours in advance so it's ready for a quick roasting.

4 quails

1 red chilli, deseeded and finely
   chopped

2 garlic cloves, crushed

15 g (½ oz) fresh root ginger,
   peeled and grated

2 tablespoons clear honey

1 tablespoon light muscovado
   sugar

juice of 1 lime

2 tablespoons vegetable oil, plus
   extra for frying

500 g (1 lb) slender sweet
   potatoes, scrubbed

salt and pepper

Use kitchen scissors or shears to cut off the wing tips from the quails, then cut through each bird on either side of the backbone. Discard the backbone and flatten each quail. Place them in a shallow ovenproof dish into which they fit quite snugly.

Mix the chilli with the garlic, ginger, honey, sugar, lime juice, salt and pepper and the 2 tablespoons oil. Pour the mixture over the quail, cover with clingfilm and chill until ready to cook.

Uncover the quail and roast in a preheated oven, 200°C (400°F), Gas Mark 6, for 20 minutes until the quail is just beginning to brown.

Meanwhile, slice the sweet potatoes as thinly as possible. Heat oil to a depth of 2 cm (¾ inch) in a large, heavy-based frying pan until a slice of potato sizzles on the surface. Fry the potatoes in 2 batches until golden. Drain on kitchen paper.

Transfer the quail and chips to warm serving plates and spoon over the juices.

spicy maple ribs

PREP: 10 MINUTES, PLUS
MARINATING
COOKING TIME: 1½–1¾ HOURS
SERVES: 4

1.25 kg (2½ lb) meaty pork spare
    ribs
100 ml (3½ fl oz) maple syrup
2 garlic cloves, crushed
3 tablespoons white wine vinegar
3 tablespoons tomato paste
finely grated rind and juice of
    1 lemon
1 red chilli, deseeded and finely
    chopped
½ teaspoon smoked paprika
salt
lemon or lime halves, to serve

Lengthy cooking ensures that the pork falls easily from
the bone and the juices bake to a deliciously dark,
sticky glaze. Just remember to baste several times
during cooking. Serve the ribs with a watercress
or another dark leaf salad and baked potatoes or
chunky chips.

Arrange the meat in a single layer in a shallow, non-metallic dish. Beat
together the maple syrup, garlic, wine vinegar, tomato paste, lemon rind
and juice, chilli and paprika.

Pour the mixture over the ribs, turning them until they are completely
coated. Cover and marinate in the refrigerator for up to 24 hours.

Transfer the ribs to a shallow roasting tin and pour over the excess
marinade from the dish. Season lightly with salt and bake in a preheated
oven, 180°C (350°F), Gas Mark 4, for 1½–1¾ hours, basting occasionally
with the juices, until the meat is tender and the juices are thick and sticky.

Transfer the ribs and the juices to serving plates and serve with lemon
or lime halves.

teriyaki salmon
on noodles

PREP: 10 MINUTES, PLUS
MARINATING
COOKING TIME: 6 MINUTES
SERVES: 4

4 skinless salmon fillets, about
   125 g (4 oz) each
2 tablespoons soy sauce
1 tablespoon dry sherry
2 tablespoons soft brown sugar
2 garlic cloves, crushed
1 teaspoon grated fresh root
   ginger
1 tablespoon sesame oil
2 tablespoons sesame seeds
2 spring onions, chopped
250 g (8 oz) dried rice noodles,
   cooked according to packet
   instructions
3 tablespoons chopped fresh
   coriander

Put the salmon fillets on a foil-lined grill pan. In a small bowl mix together the soy sauce, sherry, sugar, garlic, ginger, half the oil and 2 tablespoons water. Brush half the marinade over the salmon and set aside for 10 minutes.

Cook the salmon under a preheated hot grill for 5–6 minutes, turning it halfway through the cooking time and brushing with a little more of the marinade.

Meanwhile, heat the remaining oil in a saucepan, add the sesame seeds and spring onions and fry for 1 minute.

Cook the noodles according to the instructions on the packet. Add the noodles and any remaining marinade to the saucepan and heat through. Stir in the coriander. Serve the salmon on a bed of noodles.

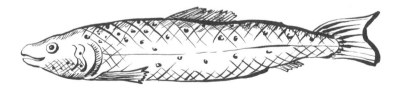

crispy aromatic
duck

PREP: 20 MINUTES, PLUS
MARINATING AND STANDING
COOKING TIME: 50 MINUTES
SERVES: 8 AS A STARTER

1 Gressingham duck, about 1 kg
   (2 lb), halved and flattened
   slightly
3 litres (5 pints) vegetable stock

Marinade
1 tablespoon five spice powder
1 tablespoon ground ginger
2 star anise
2 tablespoons Sichuan
   peppercorns
2 tablespoons black peppercorns
3 tablespoons cumin seeds
3 tablespoons fennel seeds
1 tablespoon shoyu or tamari
   sauce
6 slices fresh root ginger, peeled
   and crushed
6 spring onions, chopped
2 bay leaves, crumbled

Combine the marinade ingredients and rub the mixture into the duck halves. Cover and leave overnight or for at least a couple of hours in the refrigerator.

Bring the stock to the boil in a large saucepan. Gently lower the duck into the pan, then bring the stock back to the boil. Turn down the heat to low, cover the pan and simmer for 45 minutes.

Leave the duck to cool in the liquid for 10–15 minutes then remove it with a slotted spoon and pat dry on kitchen paper.

Place the duck halves, skin side up, on a rack set in a roasting tin. Put the tin under a preheated very hot grill and grill for 3–5 minutes to brown the skin. Watch closely so that it does not burn.

Remove the duck and blot the excess fat from the skin. Leave the duck to cool slightly then flake the meat with 2 forks.

Serve with Chinese pancakes, sliced cucumber, sliced spring onions and some hoisin sauce diluted with a little stock.

Mike Robinson's

rabbit with shallots, rosemary and garlic with parsley mash

' In Britain we eat less rabbit than any other European nation. Why? Certainly during the Second World War virtually everyone in rural areas lived on them. Rabbit is incredibly delicious. It is low in fat, it is a white meat, and it does not have a strong, gamey flavour. It is also cheap to buy – and remember, wild rabbit is organic in the true sense of the word! In my book, rabbit is superior to chicken in nearly every way and should be a lot more popular. Everyone who can make a casserole can cook rabbit successfully, which is why I included this lovely rich stew. '

PREP: 50 MINUTES
COOKING TIME: 2–3 HOURS
SERVES: 4

1 tablespoon plain flour
1 large rabbit, cut into 8 pieces
    (ask your butcher to do this)
25 g (1 oz) butter, plus 15 g (½ oz)
    softened
2 tablespoons olive oil
125 g (4 oz) smoked bacon or
    pancetta lardons
16 shallots
4 plump garlic cloves, finely
    chopped, plus extra whole,
    unpeeled cloves (optional)
1 bottle of red wine, such as
    Burgundy or Pinot Noir
1 large sprig of rosemary
1 tablespoon cornflour
salt and pepper
1 tablespoon chopped parsley,
    to serve

Parsley mash
1kg (2 lb) floury potatoes, such as
    Maris Piper or King Edward,
    peeled and cut into 2.5 cm
    (1 inch) dice
50 g (2 oz) butter, softened
3–4 tablespoons hot milk
2 tablespoons curly parsley,
    finely chopped

Season the flour with salt and pepper and roll the rabbit pieces in the flour to cover.

Heat the butter and the oil in a heavy-based casserole over a medium heat and gently fry the rabbit until the pieces are golden-brown all over (do this in batches). Remove the rabbit from the casserole and reserve. Add the bacon to the casserole and cook gently.

Meanwhile, peel the shallots. Chop half of them finely and leave the rest whole. Add them all to the bacon, together with the chopped garlic. Cook for 5–6 minutes until everything is browned and the bottom of the casserole is sticky.

Increase the heat and add a glass of red wine. Scrape the burned bits away from the base of the casserole and stir them into the wine.

Add the rabbit, packing it in tightly. Lay the rosemary on top and scatter over the whole garlic cloves (if used). Add wine until it covers the rabbit.

Cover the casserole and cook in a preheated oven, 180°C (350°F), Gas Mark 4, for 1½ hours for farmed rabbit or 2½ hours for wild rabbit.

Meanwhile, make the parsley mash. Cook the potatoes in lightly salted, boiling water for 15–20 minutes or until tender. Drain thoroughly and shake until they are dry and fluffy. Mash until smooth. Mix in the butter, milk and parsley and season to taste with salt and pepper.

When the rabbit is so tender that it falls off the bone, transfer the meat to a serving dish. Mix the cornflour with the softened butter and stir into the sauce to thicken it. Pour the sauce over the rabbit and scatter over the shallots and garlic. Sprinkle with parsley and serve with the mash.

love hearts

PREP: 30 MINUTES, PLUS COOLING
COOKING TIME: 18–20 MINUTES
MAKES: 12 CAKES

150 g (5 oz) unsalted butter,
    softened
150 g (5 oz) caster sugar
175 g (6 oz) self-raising flour
3 eggs
1 teaspoon vanilla extract

To decorate
200 g (7 oz) icing sugar
4–5 teaspoons rosewater or
    lemon juice
100 g (3½ oz) red ready-to-roll
    icing
icing sugar, for dusting
6 tablespoons strawberry jam

Line a 12-section cake tin with paper cases. Put the butter, sugar, flour, eggs and vanilla extract in a mixing bowl and beat with a hand-held electric whisk for 1–2 minutes until light and creamy. Spoon the mixture evenly into the paper cases.

Bake the cakes in a preheated oven, 180°C (350°F), Gas Mark 4, for 18–20 minutes until risen and just firm to the touch. Transfer to a wire rack to cool.

When the cakes are cold, put the icing sugar in a bowl and add 4 teaspoons of the rosewater or lemon juice. Mix until smooth, adding a little more liquid if necessary, until the icing is a thick paste. Spread over the tops of the fairy cakes.

Knead the red ready-to-roll icing on a surface lightly dusted with icing sugar. Roll out thickly and cut out 12 heart shapes using a small cookie cutter. Place a heart on the top of each cake.

Press the jam through a small sieve to remove the seeds or pulp. Put the sieved jam in a small piping bag fitted with a writing nozzle. Pipe small dots into the icing around the edges of each cake and pipe a line of jam around the edges of the heart.

*E*ric Lanlard's
lemon and passion fruit tart with raspberries

PREP: 30 MINUTES, PLUS CHILLING
COOKING TIME: ABOUT 1¼ HOURS
SERVES: 8–10

375 g (12 oz) pâte sucrée
2 large passion fruits
4 eggs
150 g (5 oz) caster sugar
150 ml (½ pint) double cream
grated rind and juice of 3 lemons
125 g (4 oz) fresh raspberries

To decorate
½ passion fruit
a few redcurrants
a few strawberries
slices of poached lemon
2 tablespoons apricot jam, sieved
1 tablespoon icing sugar

Roll out the pastry on a lightly floured surface and use it to line a 23 cm (9 inch) round tart tin. Chill for 20 minutes, then line the pastry case with greaseproof paper and baking beans. Place on a baking sheet and bake blind in a preheated oven, 190°C (375°F), Gas Mark 5, for 15–20 minutes until golden. Reduce the oven temperature to 150°C (300°F), Gas Mark 2.

Meanwhile, halve the passion fruits and scoop out the pulp and seeds.

Break the eggs into a large bowl, add the sugar and whisk until pale and creamy. Add the cream, lemon rind and juice and the passion fruit pulp and seeds and mix well.

Arrange the raspberries on the base of the cooked pastry case and pour over the lemon and passion fruit mixture. Bake for 1 hour or until the filling is set but still wobbly. Leave to cool.

Decorate the tart with the fruit. Brush with the apricot jam and dust lightly with icing sugar.

Ursula Ferrigno's

biscotti a forma di cuore
(heart-shaped biscuits)

‘These biscuits make my husband very happy, and he often says they are the reason he married me! They are all very tasty and do-able. I hope you like them ... The Italians are famously passionate and romantic, and making biscuits or other foods in heart shapes is very popular. I think these would be perfect for St Valentine's Day, for someone's birthday or for part of a special occasion. You can, of course, make the biscuits any shape. Eat them with ice cream, dip them into *Vin Santo* or even eat them with a coffee in the afternoon as a *merenda* or snack.’

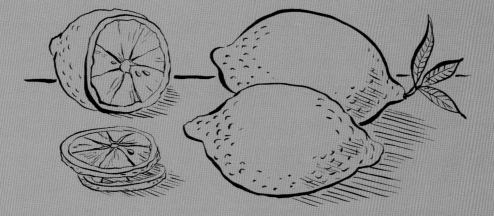

125 g (4 oz) unsalted butter, plus
    extra for greasing
150 g (5 oz) caster sugar, plus
    extra to sprinkle
1 large egg, separated
250 g (8 oz) plain flour or Italian
    '00' plain flour
finely grated rind of 1 unwaxed
    lemon

Cream together the butter and sugar until light and fluffy. Add the egg yolk and beat well, then stir in the flour and lemon rind.

Knead the dough lightly and shape into a ball. Wrap in clingfilm and chill for 20 minutes to make it firm and easier to roll.

Divide the mixture in half and return half to the refrigerator. Roll out the dough on a lightly floured surface to about 5 mm (¼ inch) thick. Use a 6 cm (2½ inch) heart-shaped biscuit cutter to cut out the biscuits. Brush away any excess flour on the biscuits. Repeat with the remaining dough.

Put the biscuits on 2 lightly greased baking sheets, spacing them well apart. Lightly beat the egg white with 1 tablespoon water and use the mixture to glaze the biscuits. Sprinkle with sugar.

Bake the biscuits in a preheated oven, 180°C (350°F), Gas Mark 4, for 15 minutes until light brown. Transfer to wire racks and leave to cool.

valentine martini

PREP: 5 MINUTES
NO COOK
SERVES: 2

4 measures raspberry vodka

12 raspberries

1 measure fresh lime juice

dash of sugar syrup

ice cubes

To decorate:

4 raspberries

lime twists

Put all the ingredients into a cocktail shaker and add some ice cubes.

Shake then double strain into chilled cocktail glasses. Decorate each one with 2 raspberries on a cocktail stick and a lime twist.

honeymoon

PREP: 5 MINUTES
NO COOK
SERVES: 2

crushed ice

2 measures maple syrup or clear honey

50 ml (2 fl oz) fresh lime juice

2 measures orange juice

2 measures apple juice

cocktail cherries, to decorate

Put some crushed ice in a cocktail shaker and add the maple syrup or honey, lime juice, orange juice and apple juice.

Shake well and strain into chilled cocktail glasses. Decorate each one with a cherry on a cocktail stick.

> ❝ I chose this recipe as my grandmother, who had breast cancer, always used to make them for me and my brother when we visited her and my grandfather in South Africa each year. It became a bit of a tradition. I could smell the sweet scent of the cookies as soon as we opened the door and they'd be sitting on the kitchen counter waiting for us. She then passed the recipe on so we can continue to remember her and what an amazing cook she was! ❞
>
> **Tessa Kottler**, **Breast Cancer Care employee, grandmother diagnosed 1980**

surprise kisses ✽

PREP: 15 MINUTES
COOKING TIME: 30–35 MINUTES
MAKES: 26–28 BISCUITS

4 egg whites
375 g (12 oz) golden caster sugar
¼ teaspoon cream of tartar
1 teaspoon vanilla extract
200 g (7 oz) good-quality plain
    chocolate, coarsley grated

Beat the egg whites until stiff then add the sugar a spoonful at a time. Add the cream of tartar and vanilla extract with the last of the sugar, and fold in the chocolate.

Drop heaped dessertspoonfuls of the mixture on to 2 lightly greased baking sheets, spacing the spoonfuls well apart. Bake in a preheated oven, 150°C (300°F), Gas Mark 2, for 30–35 minutes, swapping the baking sheets round halfway through cooking.

sweet treats

This is the chapter that will satisfy the sweetest tooth. Here you'll find a wonderful selection of cakes, biscuits, desserts and sauces that can be prepared for any occasion. From something sweet to enjoy with a morning coffee, to family puds and teatime treats, there's no shortage of mouth-watering recipes.

Antony Worrall Thompson's

green tea ice cream

6 Everyone loves ice cream. I hope this recipe will uplift the spirits and at the same time raise loads of money for Breast Cancer Care's range of terrific free services which deserve everyone's support. Thank you for asking me to be a part of it. 9

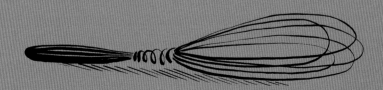

PREP: 15 MINUTES
COOKING TIME: 8 MINUTES
SERVES: 4

2 egg yolks
200 ml (7 fl oz) milk
2 tablespoons sugar
2 tablespoons jasmine green tea
200 ml (7 fl oz) double cream

Lightly whisk the egg yolks in a saucepan. Add the milk and sugar to the pan and mix well.

Heat the mixture over a low heat, stirring constantly, and when the mixture has thickened, remove from the heat and stand the base of the pan in ice-cold water to cool the mixture.

Mix the green tea with 100 ml (3½ fl oz) hot water and add this to the egg mixture, stirring well as it cools.

Add the cream to the mixture and mix well together. Strain through a fine sieve.

Freeze the mixture in an ice-cream maker, following the manufacturer's instructions. Alternatively, transfer to a freezer proof container and freeze for 2 hours, then mash the crystals with a fork. Return to the freezer for a further 2 hours, mash again, then allow the ice cream to freeze solid.

thyme, orange and chocolate
shortbread

PREP: 15 MINUTES, PLUS CHILLING
COOKING TIME: 20 MINUTES
MAKES: 25 BISCUITS

1 tablespoon chopped thyme
50 g (2 oz) caster sugar
150 g (5 oz) milk or white
    chocolate, chopped
250 g (8 oz) plain flour
100 g (3½ oz) rice flour
finely grated rind of 1 orange
200 g (7 oz) lightly salted butter,
    diced

Reserve 1 teaspoon of the chopped thyme. Sprinkle the remainder over 25 g (1 oz) of the sugar on a chopping board and press the thyme into the sugar with the side of the knife. Set aside. Melt the chocolate in a small bowl set over a pan of simmering water.

Sift the flour and rice flour into a mixing bowl. Add the reserved thyme, orange rind and butter and rub in with your fingertips until the mixture resembles coarse breadcrumbs.

Stir in the remaining sugar and the melted chocolate and mix with a round-bladed knife until the mixture starts to form a dough. Use your hands to bring the mixture together then turn it on to the work surface.

Shape the mixture into a thick log, about 30 cm (12 inches) long. Roll it up in greaseproof paper and chill for 1 hour.

Roll the log in the herb sugar. Cut it across into thick slices and space the slices slightly apart on 2 lightly oiled baking sheets. Bake in a preheated oven, 180°C (350°F), Gas Mark 4, for about 20 minutes until beginning to turn pale golden. Transfer to a wire rack to cool.

Fern Britton's
caramelized apricot sauce

PREP: 15 MINUTES
COOKING TIME: 10 MINUTES
SERVES: 8–10

250 g (8 oz) caster sugar
150 ml (¼ pint) cold water
410 g (13½ oz) can apricots in
   syrup, drained

This is delicious drizzled over ice cream or served with Carrot Cake (see pages 150-151).

Put the sugar in a saucepan, add 2 tablespoons of the water and bring to the boil. Cook until it turns a dark caramel colour.

Pour in the remaining the water and stand back because the mixture will splutter and splash. Allow the syrup to boil and then leave to cool a little.

Liquidize the apricots until smooth and add enough cooled syrup to give a nice caramel-flavoured sauce. Leave to cool completely.

❝ We have known many people who have been affected by this dreadful disease; we hope this book will be a real success, and go some way to helping all those involved. ❞

Phil Vickery and Fern Britton

iced lavender
loaves

PREP: 20–25 MINUTES
COOKING TIME: 20–25 MINUTES
MAKES: 8 LOAVES

1 tablespoon lavender flowers
(about 8 flowerheads), plus
extra to decorate
175 g (6 oz) unsalted butter,
softened
175 g (6 oz) golden caster sugar
3 eggs
175 g (6 oz) self-raising flour
1 teaspoon baking powder
finely grated rind of 1 lemon

Glacé icing
75 g (3 oz) icing sugar
2 teaspoons lemon or lime juice
1–2 drops lilac food colouring

These loaves would be great to sell at a cake stall in aid of the Lavender Trust at **Breast Cancer Care**. Every March, the Lavender Trust runs its own campaign, Lavender Week. The aim of the week is to raise awareness of the issues facing younger women with breast cancer. The Lavender Trust also aims to raise vital funds to enable greater access to the information and support which Breast Cancer Care has developed specifically for this age group. To find out how you can get involved next March, visit www.lavendertrust.org.uk

Lightly grease and line 8 individual loaf tins, each with a 200 g (7 oz) capacity. Put half the lavender flowers in a bowl with the butter, sugar, eggs, flour, baking powder and lemon rind and beat until smooth. Spoon the mixture into the prepared tins and bake in a preheated oven, 180°C (350°F), Gas Mark 4, for 20–25 minutes. Transfer to a wire rack to cool.

Put the icing sugar and lemon or lime juice in a bowl and beat until smooth. Stir in the reserved lavender flowers and the food colouring. Spoon the icing over the cooled loaves and decorate with extra flowers.

> 'Something tasty and with a little zing was always welcome when I had that metallic taste during chemotherapy. This is quick and easy enough to make as little gifts for special people – I use nice wee tumblers instead of jars. '
>
> **Nan McDonald,**
> **Breast Cancer Care volunteer, diagnosed 1996**

sunshine
lemon curd ✻

PREP: 15 MINUTES
COOKING TIME: 4–4½ MINUTES
MAKES: 600 ML (1 PINT)

2 eggs, plus 2 yolks
250 g (8 oz) caster sugar
finely grated rind of 3 lemons and
    125 ml (4 fl oz) juice
125 g (4 oz) unsalted butter,
    melted

This lemon curd makes a tasty filling for meringue nests, pavlova rolls or pastry cases but is perhaps best of all on dropped scones, hot from the griddle.

Whisk together the eggs and egg yolks with the sugar and lemon rind and juice.

Beat in the butter and cook in a microwave on high for 2 minutes. Beat well and cook for a further 2–2½ minutes, then stir. The curd should be thick enough to coat the back of a wooden spoon.

Pour into small, clean dry jars, seal and cool.

Lisa Faulkner
julie's sunshine shorties

" I'm supporting this cookbook because my mum died of cancer when I was 16. She is the biggest inspiration to me, and I feel so blessed to have been her daughter. Biscuits are real "comfort food", and sometimes we all need a bit of that! This is a really simple recipe, which my mum used to make all the time. Really good when you want to feel like a "domestic goddess" without the hard work! "

PREP: 10 MINUTES
COOKING TIME: 10 MINUTES
MAKES: 24 BISCUITS

125 g (4 oz) butter
125 g (4 oz) sugar
1 teaspoon golden syrup
1 teaspoon bicarbonate of soda
1 teaspoon boiling water
125 g (4 oz) porridge oats
125 g (4 oz) self-raising flour

Put the butter, sugar, syrup, bicarbonate of soda and water in a saucepan and melt over a gentle heat.

Add the oats and flour and mix well, then remove from the heat.

Lightly oil a baking sheet. Place teaspoon-size balls of the mixture on the baking sheet, spacing them well apart.

Bake in a preheated oven, 180°C (350°C), Gas Mark 4, for 8–10 minutes.

lemon
drizzle cake

PREP: 20 MINUTES
COOKING TIME: 20–25 MINUTES
SERVES: 8

5 eggs

125 g (4 oz) sugar

pinch of salt

125 g (4 oz) plain flour

1 teaspoon baking powder

finely grated rind of 1 lemon

1 tablespoon lemon juice

100 g (3½ oz) melted butter,
    cooled

crème fraîche or soured cream,
    to serve

Syrup

250 g (8 oz) icing sugar

125 ml (4 fl oz) lemon juice

finely grated rind of 1 lemon

seeds scraped from 1 vanilla pod

Line and grease the base and sides of a 20 cm (8 inch) square cake tin. Put the eggs, sugar and salt in a large, heatproof bowl and place over a pan of barely simmering water. Beat the mixture with a hand-held electric mixer for 2–3 minutes or until it triples in volume and thickens to the consistency of lightly whipped cream. Remove from the heat.

Sift in the flour and baking powder, add the lemon rind and juice and drizzle the butter down the sides of the bowl. Fold in gently using a large metal spoon. Pour the mixture into the prepared cake tin and cook in a preheated oven, 180°C (350°F), Gas Mark 4, for 20–25 minutes or until it is risen, golden and coming away from the sides of the pan.

Meanwhile, make the syrup. Place all the syrup ingredients in a small pan and heat gently until the sugar has dissolved. Increase the heat and boil rapidly for 4–5 minutes or until you have a light syrup. Leave to cool a little.

Remove the cake from the oven and leave it to cool for 5 minutes. Make holes over the surface with a skewer and drizzle over two-thirds of the warm syrup. Leave the cake in the tin to cool and absorb the syrup.

Carefully remove the cake from the tin and peel away the lining paper. Place it on a dish and serve in squares or slices with a spoonful of crème fraîche or soured cream and an extra drizzle of syrup.

> '   I was first diagnosed with breast cancer in January 2002 and since then have had two recurrences. I have been physically cancer free for two years now, but mentally the cancer colours my life. It makes me look for the best in everything and helps me enjoy life to the full. I have chosen lime cheesecake because when I was ill I could enlist the aid of my children to make it and because of its sweet but sharp taste. '
>
> **Pauline Davidson, diagnosed 2002**

lime
cheesecake ✽

PREP: 15 MINUTES, PLUS CHILLING
NO COOK
SERVES: 6–8

200 g (7 oz) ginger biscuits,
    crushed
50 g (2 oz) unsalted butter, melted
finely grated rind and juice
    of 2 limes
500 g (1 lb) mascarpone cheese
50 g (2 oz) icing sugar
1 chocolate flake, crushed

Lightly butter a 20 cm (8 inch) springform tin and line the base with buttered greaseproof paper. Mix together the biscuit crumbs and the butter and press the mixture into the base of the tin. Leave to set in the refrigerator while making the topping.

Beat together the lime rind and juice, cheese and icing sugar in a large bowl to make a smooth cream.

Pour the mixture over the crumb base and chill for at least 45 minutes.

Just before serving, sprinkle over the crushed chocolate flakes.

coconut frosted
angel cake

PREP: 30 MINUTES
COOKING TIME: 30 MINUTES
SERVES: 10–12

vegetable oil, for brushing
150 g (5 oz) plain flour, plus extra
    for dusting
8 egg whites
1 teaspoon cream of tartar
225 g (7½ oz) caster sugar
2 teaspoons vanilla extract
toasted coconut shavings,
    to decorate

Coconut icing
75 ml (3 fl oz) single cream
50 g (2 oz) creamed coconut,
    chopped
2–3 teaspoons lemon or lime
    juice
300 g (10 oz) icing sugar

Brush a 1.5 litre (2½ pint) ring tin with oil and coat with flour, tapping out the excess. Beat the egg whites in a large, thoroughly clean bowl until frothy. Add the cream of tartar and beat until peaking.

Gradually beat in the sugar, a tablespoonful at a time, beating well after each addition until the mixture is stiff and glossy. Beat in the vanilla extract with the last of the sugar.

Sift the flour into the bowl and gently fold it into the mixture, using a large metal spoon. Turn the mixture into the tin and level the surface. Bake in a preheated oven, 160°C (325°F), Gas Mark 3, for about 25 minutes or until the cake is firm to the touch and a skewer inserted into the centre comes out clean.

Invert the cake on to a wire rack but don't remove the tin. When cool, loosen the edges of the tin and turn the cake out on to a flat plate.

Meanwhile, make the icing. Put the cream and creamed coconut in a small saucepan and heat gently until the coconut has melted. Turn it into a bowl and whisk in the lemon or lime juice and icing sugar until it is fairly thick and smooth.

Spread the icing over the cake and scatter with the toasted coconut shavings.

german apple
cake ✳

PREP: 35 MINUTES, PLUS
DRAINING
COOKING TIME: 45 MINUTES
SERVES: 8–10

125 g (4 oz) unsalted butter,
  softened, or margarine, diced,
  plus extra for greasing
4 large cooking apples, such as
  Bramley, peeled, cored and
  thinly sliced
2 lemons
250 g (8 oz) self-raising flour
125 g (4 oz) caster sugar
1 large egg
2–3 teaspoons vanilla extract
whipped cream, to serve

Icing
200 g (7 oz) icing sugar
2–3 teaspoons lemon juice

Lightly grease a 20 x 5 cm (8 x 2 inch) loose-based cake tin. Gently cook the apples in the juice of one lemon, adding a little water if necessary. Drain the cooked slices for at least 30 minutes and cool.

Meanwhile, put the flour in a mixing bowl, make a well in the centre and add the sugar, egg and vanilla. Mix with a fork, add the diced butter or margarine and rub in with your fingertips. Knead to make a dough.

Turn out the dough on a lightly floured surface. Roll out two-thirds and line the base of the tin. Add the apple. Roll out the remaining pastry and cover the apples, pressing the edges of the pastry firmly together.

Bake the cake in a preheated oven, 160°C (325°F), Gas Mark 3, for 40–45 minutes or until light brown. Leave it to cool in the tin, then turn it upside down on a serving plate. To make the icing, mix the icing sugar with the juice of the remaining lemon to a thick consistency. Spread the icing over the warm cake and serve cold with whipped cream.

espresso tart

with chocolate pastry

PREP: 15 MINUTES, PLUS CHILLING
COOKING TIME: ABOUT 1 HOUR
SERVES: 8

Pastry

200 g (7 oz) flour

40 g (1½ oz) good-quality cocoa
    powder

50 g (2 oz) golden caster sugar

150 g (5 oz) butter, diced

1 large egg, beaten

2–3 tablespoons iced water

Filling

450 ml (¾ pint) double cream

3 eggs

125 g (4 oz) golden caster sugar

2 tablespoons instant espresso
    coffee powder

25 g (1 oz) plain chocolate, grated

This rich, indulgent tart is surprisingly simple to make.
For an extra treat, you could decorate the top with
chocolate coffee beans.

Make the pastry. Sift the flour and cocoa powder into a bowl. Add the
sugar and butter and mix with the fingertips until the mixture resembles
breadcrumbs.

Add the egg and just enough iced water to make a firm dough. Roll out
the pastry and line a 23 cm (9 inch) tart tin. Chill for 30 minutes, then
trim the edges.

Bake the pastry case blind in a preheated oven, 180°C (350°F), Gas
Mark 4, for 15 minutes. Remove the beans and paper or foil and return
the tart to the oven for a further 10 minutes.

Heat the cream until it boils. Whisk the eggs, sugar and coffee powder
then pour the hot cream over them, stirring continually. Pour the mixture
through a fine sieve and then into the tart case.

Bake the tart for 30–35 minutes or until set. Remove it from the oven
and sprinkle with grated dark chocolate. Leave to cool before serving.

Romola Garai's
snooklish sauce

PREP: 5 MINUTES
NO COOK
SERVES: 4

2 tablespoons butter-like spread
1½ tablespoons golden syrup
1 tablespoon muscovado sugar
2 tablespoons cocoa powder

Put the butter spread in a saucepan, add the syrup and sugar and melt over a low heat, stirring, until they come together.

Add the cocoa, stirring, until the sauce starts to thicken. Enjoy with anything or, even better, on its own, but use while still warm as it sets hard when cold.

  6 This is my recipe for a vegan-friendly chocolate sauce. It is really good, and the rest of the family lapped it up in spite of it having no dairy, usually a prerequisite for us to enjoy anything. Somehow it developed the name "Snooklish Sauce" but nobody seems to know how! **9**

*F*ern Britton's
queen of puddings

❝ This is one of Fern's favourite puddings. When I was an apprentice we would always finish the top with greengage and raspberry jams – the contrasting colours are essential. The secret is to not overcook the custard. Any cake or breadcrumbs will do, I just love buttery Madeira cake. This, along with egg custard tart, I think, is the ultimate comfort food experience. ❞

Phil Vickery and Fern Britton

PREP: 25 MINUTES
COOKING TIME: 50–55 MINUTES
SERVES: 4–6

600 ml (1 pint) milk
1 vanilla pod, split
3 large eggs, separated
125 g (4 oz) caster sugar, plus
    extra to sprinkle
75 g (3 oz) Madeira cake crumbs
    or fine breadcrumbs
pinch of freshly grated nutmeg
finely grated rind of 1 lemon
pinch of cream of tartar
75 g (3 oz) icing sugar, sieved
2 tablespoons greengage or
    green rhubarb jam
2 tablespoons raspberry jam
double cream, to serve

Lightly oil a 23 cm (9 inch) square ceramic baking dish 6 cm (2½ inches) deep. Put the milk and vanilla pod in a heavy-based saucepan and bring to the boil.

Meanwhile, whisk together the egg yolks and 25 g (1 oz) caster sugar until pale and frothy. When the milk is boiling, pour it on to the egg yolks and whisk well. Strain into a large jug and keep warm.

Mix together the cake or breadcrumbs, nutmeg and lemon rind in a large bowl. Pour on the hot milk and whisk together. Carefully pour into the prepared baking dish, cover with foil and cook in a preheated oven, 160°C (325°F), Gas Mark 3, for about 40-45 minutes. Take care when cooking because it will set then curdle very quickly. It should be just set.

Remove the pudding from the oven and leave to cool for 15 minutes. Increase the oven temperature to 220°C (425°F), Gas Mark 7.

Make the meringue. Put the egg whites in a mixing bowl, add the cream of tartar and whisk on half speed. When they are thick and foamy, but not splitting, add the remaining caster sugar and whisk again on medium speed until shiny and glossy. Do not over-beat. Remove the bowl from the machine and carefully fold in the icing sugar.

Fit a 1 cm (½ inch) plain piping tube on a piping bag and fill it with the finished meringue. Pipe diagonal lines across the warm custard, leaving 2 cm (¾ inch) gaps between the lines. Repeat in the opposite direction so you end up with diamond-shaped custard holes.

Fill alternate holes with the two jams. Sprinkle with a little caster sugar and bake in the oven for 7–10 minutes or until the pudding is a deep beige colour and the meringue is crisp. Serve with double cream.

> 'A huge family favourite borrowed from my Auntie Maureen. This always flies off the plate and is easy and quick to make!'
> **Susan Woodcock,** touched by breast cancer

crème caramel
meringue ✿

PREP: 20 MINUTES, PLUS CHILLING
COOKING TIME: 1½ HOURS
SERVES: 6

125 g (4 oz) granulated sugar
150 ml (¼ pint) milk
275 ml (9 fl oz) single cream
4 large eggs
40 g (1½ oz) soft brown sugar
3 drops of vanilla extract

Filling
200 ml (7 fl oz) double cream
3 good-quality, ready-made
    meringue nests, roughly
    broken
200 g (7 oz) fresh fruit, such as
    raspberries or strawberries, or
    canned mandarin oranges,
    drained

Make the caramel. Put the granulated sugar in a small, heavy-based saucepan and heat, stirring, until melted. Remove the saucepan from the heat and add 1 tablespoon hot water. Stir until smooth, then pour into a 900 ml (1½ pint) ring mould.

Put the milk and single cream into a saucepan and heat gently. Blend together the eggs, brown sugar and vanilla extract in a large bowl. When the milk and cream reach steaming point, pour them into the sugar and egg mixture and whisk until blended. Pour the mixture into the ring mould and transfer it to a shallow baking tin. Pour in cold water until it reaches halfway up the sides of mould and cook in a preheated oven, 150°C (300°F), Gas Mark 2, for 1 hour. Remove from the oven, leave to cool, then chill.

When you are ready to serve, stand the ring mould in about 1 cm (½ inch) hot water and run a palette knife around the inner and outer edges. Put a serving plate on top and invert to release the crème caramel. Whip the cream and stir in the meringue pieces and two-thirds of the fruit, Spoon into centre of the caramel, decorate with the remaining fruit and serve.

fresh ginger and pineapple
teabread

PREP: 20 MINUTES
COOKING TIME: ABOUT 1 HOUR
SERVES: 10

65 g (2½ oz) fresh root ginger
½ small pineapple, about 350 g
   (11½ oz)
150 g (5 oz) unsalted butter,
   softened
150 g (5 oz) golden caster sugar
3 eggs
225 g (7½ oz) self-raising flour
1 teaspoon baking powder
65 g (2½ oz) icing sugar

Fresh root ginger tastes just as spicy and vibrant in sweet dishes as it does in savoury ones. Use a very fresh piece so it's really aromatic and juicy.

Line the base and sides of a 1 kg (2 lb) loaf tin. Grease the paper. Peel the ginger and grate it over a plate to catch the juices.

Cut away the skin from the pineapple, halve the flesh and cut out the core. Cut 6 thin slices and roughly chop the remainder.

Put the butter, sugar, eggs, flour, baking powder and grated ginger in a bowl, reserving any ginger juices. Beat until smooth and creamy then stir in the chopped pineapple.

Turn the mixture into the tin and level the surface. Bake the cake in a preheated oven, 160°C (325°F), Gas Mark 3, for about 1 hour or until just firm to the touch and a skewer inserted into the centre comes out clean. Transfer it to a wire rack to cool.

Mix 2 teaspoons of the ginger juice with the icing sugar (make up with water if necessary) to make a thin icing. Arrange the sliced pineapple along the top of the warm cake and drizzle with the icing.

chocolate
cupcakes

PREP: 20 MINUTES
COOKING TIME: 20 MINUTES
MAKES: 12 CAKES

175 g (6 oz) unsalted butter,
   softened
125 g (4 oz) caster sugar
125 g (4 oz) self-raising flour
3 eggs
125 g (4 oz) ground almonds or
   hazelnuts
50 g (2 oz) unblanched hazelnuts,
   coarsely chopped and toasted
75 g (3 oz) white chocolate,
   chopped
75 g (3 oz) milk chocolate,
   chopped

Butter icing
250 g (8 oz) unsalted butter,
   softened
50 g (2 oz) caster sugar
125 g (4 oz) icing sugar
2 teaspoons lemon juice

Line a 12-section muffin tin with paper cases. Put the butter, caster sugar, flour, eggs, and ground almonds or hazelnuts into a bowl and beat with a hand-held electric beater for 1–2 minutes until pale and creamy.

Reserve a handful of the chopped unblanched hazelnuts for decoration. Add the remainder to the creamed mixture with the white and milk chocolates, mix together and spoon into the paper cases.

Bake the cakes in a preheated oven, 180°C (350°F), Gas Mark 4, for about 20 minutes until they are risen and just firm to the touch. Transfer to a wire rack to cool.

Make the icing. Beat together the butter, sugars and lemon juice in a bowl until pale and fluffy. Spread the icing over the cakes with a small spatula and decorate with the reserved nuts.

‘ This cake has always been a favourite with my family. I used to make it when on chemotherapy as it was quick and easy and always nice with a cup of tea when friends popped in to see how I was. ’

Margaret Knight, **Breast Cancer Care volunteer, diagnosed 1992**

quick fruit
cake ❋

PREP: 10 MINUTES, PLUS COOLING
COOKING TIME: 1¼–1½ HOURS
SERVES: 8–10

350 g (11½ oz) luxury mixed dried
    fruit
125 g (4 oz) light muscovado
    sugar
125 g (4 oz) unsalted butter or
    margarine
1 teaspoon ground mixed spice
2 eggs, beaten
250 g (8 oz) self-raising flour

Put the dried fruit, sugar, butter or margarine and mixed spice in a saucepan with 150 ml (¼ pint) water. Simmer for 10 minutes until the juices are syrupy and then leave to cool for at least 20 minutes.

Add the eggs and stir in the flour.

Turn the mixture into a lightly greased 15 cm (6 inch) cake tin and bake in a preheated oven, 150°C (300°F), Gas Mark 2, for about 1¼ hours. Test with skewer. Remove from the tin and allow to cool if you can, although it is lovely warm.

strawberry
cream cakes

PREP: 30 MINUTES
COOKING TIME: 18–20 MINUTES
MAKES: 12 CAKES

12 home-made or shop bought
   vanilla cupcakes
300 g (10 oz) small strawberries
150 ml (¼ pint) double cream
2 teaspoons caster sugar
½ teaspoon vanilla extract
4–6 tablespoons redcurrant jelly

Make this recipe to sell at your Strawberry Tea party and raise funds for people affected by breast cancer. Every year, the charity encourages people to embrace the Wimbledon Spirit by holding a Strawberry Tea in aid of **Breast Cancer Care**. Anything goes, from a strawberry themed party for friends, to an afternoon picnic in the park or a strawberry cake sale.

To get involved in the charity's next Strawberry Tea Fortnight and for fundraising ideas and packs, visit www.breastcancercare.org.uk

Scoop out the centre of each cupcake with a small sharp knife. Reserve 6 of the smallest strawberries and thinly slice the remainder. Whip the cream with the sugar and vanilla extract until it holds soft peaks. Spoon a little into the centre of each cake.

Arrange the sliced strawberries, overlapping, around the edges of each cake. Halve the reserved strawberries and place a strawberry half in the centre of each cake. Heat the redcurrant jelly in a small saucepan with 2 tablespoons water until melted, then brush over the strawberries using a pastry brush. Store the cakes in a cool place until ready to serve.

> I have been making this fudge for holiday gifts for my friends for many years. It meant a lot to me to keep the tradition going this year during cancer treatment. It was just a tiny way to show my family that everything was normal.
> **Sarah Young, diagnosed 2006**

incredible
fudge ✳
– you can do it!

PREP: 10 MINUTES, PLUS SETTING
COOKING TIME: 15 MINUTES
MAKES: 1.5 KG (3 LB OZ)

150 g (5 oz) butter
750 g (1½ lb) sugar
170 g (6 oz) evaporated milk
300 g (10 oz) your favourite
    chocolate, broken into smallish
    pieces
150–200 g (5–7 oz) marshmallows
1 tablespoon vanilla extract

Put the butter, sugar and evaporated milk in a large, heavy-based saucepan and cook over a low heat until blended.

Attach the sugar thermometer to the pan and turn up the heat. Stir gently but constantly while you bring the mixture to the boil, and keep stirring until the temperature reaches 116°C (240°F). Take the pan off the heat and stir in the chocolate, then the marshmallows and finally the vanilla extract.

Pour the mixture into a lightly oiled, 23 cm (9 inch) square cake tin, working quickly while the mixture is hot. Pack it down firmly and leave to cool overnight. Turn out the fudge on a board and cut into squares.

celebrate!

Life should be full of celebrations and good food makes a great accompaniment to a happy event. Over the following pages you will discover a variety of recipes for special occasions and there are ideas for starters, main courses and desserts, so you can design a whole meal for family, friends or a partner.

the best
prawn cocktail

PREP: 15 MINUTES
COOKING TIME: 3–5 MINUTES
SERVES: 4

2 tablespoons olive oil

300 g (10 oz) raw peeled prawns

15 g (½ oz) fresh root ginger

150 ml (¼ pint) mayonnaise or
   good-quality shop-bought
   mayonnaise

3 tablespoons natural yogurt

1 tablespoon sun-dried tomato
   paste

1 teaspoon caster sugar

1 tablespoon lime juice

½ cos (romaine) lettuce

plenty of basil leaves

salt and pepper

lime wedges, to serve

This is a far better prawn cocktail than the one you will be served in most restaurants. It's made with freshly cooked prawns, and the mayonnaise has a fresh tang of lime juice and ginger. Use homemade mayonnaise or a good-quality bought one.

Heat the oil in a large frying pan, add the prawns and fry for 1–2 minutes on each side until they are deep pink. Sprinkle with a little salt and pepper then transfer to a plate to cool.

Peel and finely grate the ginger, working over a plate to catch the juice. Mix the ginger and juice in a bowl with the mayonnaise, yogurt, tomato paste, sugar and lime juice. Season to taste with salt and pepper and beat well.

Tear the lettuce leaves, put them into small serving bowls and add plenty of basil leaves to each bowl. Pile the cooled prawns on top. Spoon over the sauce and serve with lime wedges.

Lotte Duncan's
smoked salmon soup

PREP: 15 MINUTES
COOKING TIME: ABOUT
50 MINUTES
SERVES: 4–6

25 g (1 oz) butter
2 large leeks, sliced and
   thoroughly washed
1 small onion, sliced
3 potatoes, evenly sliced evenly
about 1 litre (1¾ pints) vegetable
   stock
150 ml (¼ pint) white wine
150 ml (¼ pint) double cream
175 g (6 oz) smoked salmon,
   thinly sliced
salt and pepper
chopped chives, to garnish

To serve
blue cheese
walnut soda bread

Heat the butter in a large, heavy-based saucepan and lightly fry the vegetables for about 5 minutes or until they are soft but not coloured.

Add the stock and wine to the pan, cover and simmer for about 45 minutes until the vegetables are cooked.

Transfer the soup to a blender, in batches if necessary, blend and return to the pan. Reheat, season to taste with pepper and stir in the cream.

Add the salmon, taste and, if necessary, season with a little salt.

Ladle the soup into bowls, sprinkle over the chopped chives and serve with some warm blue cheese and walnut soda bread.

beef

with red onion and olive dressing

PREP: 25 MINUTES, PLUS
FREEZING
COOKING TIME: ABOUT 5 MINUTES
SERVES: 4

1 tablespoon mixed peppercorns

1 tablespoon Sichuan
  peppercorns

1 teaspoon coriander seeds

475 g (15 oz) beef fillet

50 ml (2 fl oz) extra virgin olive oil

75 g (3 oz) lambs' lettuce

small handful of cress

100 g (3½ oz) small black olives in
  olive oil

1 small red onion, halved and
  very finely sliced

½ tablespoon soft green
  peppercorns

25 g (1 oz) peppery pecorino
  cheese shavings

3 tablespoons balsamic vinegar

Put the mixed and Sichuan peppercorns and coriander seeds into a mortar and pound with a pestle until they are coarsely ground. Sprinkle the mixture evenly over a large plate or chopping board.

Rub the beef with 1 tablespoon of the olive oil, then roll it over the pepper mix until the surface is completely encrusted.

Heat a dry frying pan until it is very hot and quickly sear the beef, turning it frequently, for about 5 minutes until it is blackened all over. Remove the beef from the heat, wrap it tightly in foil and put it in the freezer for about 1 hour.

When the beef is firm and beginning to freeze remove it from the freezer and put it on a chopping board. Use a sharp knife to slice the meat as thinly as possible – you are aiming for wafer-thin slices. Arrange the slices in a single layer on 4 large serving plates and put the lambs' lettuce, cress and black olives on top. Scatter with the red onion slices, green peppercorns and pecorino. Cover lightly and set aside until the beef reaches room temperature.

Before serving, drizzle the beef with the remaining olive oil and the balsamic vinegar.

tagliatelle
with shaved truffles

PREP: 5 MINUTES
COOKING TIME: 3 MINUTES
SERVES: 4

300 g (10 oz) fresh tagliatelle

75 g (3 oz) unsalted butter, diced

40 g (1½ oz) Parmesan cheese,
   freshly grated

1 small white or black truffle

salt and pepper

Truffles are hugely expensive, particularly the white (alba) ones, and they are best served simply shaved over pasta with nothing but the best Parmesan cheese. A more affordable alternative is to drizzle fresh pasta with truffle oil.

Bring a large saucepan of lightly salted water to the boil. Add the pasta and cook for 2–3 minutes or according to packet instructions until just tender. Drain and return to the saucepan.

Dot the butter over the pasta, stir in the Parmesan and season with salt and pepper.

Pile the pasta on to warm serving plates. Use a potato peeler or small mandolin slice to shave the truffle over the pasta and serve immediately.

Simon Rimmer's
fish stew with brandy

"I've always had a love of Spanish food – patatas bravas, chorizo, paella, boquerones and the like, but this is my absolute favourite dish. It's a big hearty stew, packed full of yummy fish, the kind you want to eat with your fingers and the best bit for me is the smell – it makes me salivate as I imagine myself on a harbour, cheeky glass of rioja and elbows deep in fish stew."

PREP: 45 MINUTES
COOKING TIME: 1 HOUR
SERVES: 6

750 g (1½ lb) fish and shellfish,
    such as salmon, cod, clams
    and mussels
200 g (7 oz) new potatoes, cooked
200 g (7 oz) carrots, sliced and
    cooked
200 g (7 oz) fine beans, sliced and
    cooked
2 tomatoes, skinned, deseeded
    and chopped
2 tablespoons chopped parsley
2 tablespoons lemon juice
6 tablespoons double cream
salt and pepper

Sauce
50 g (2 oz) butter
5 shallots, peeled and halved
2 large carrots, roughly chopped
5 leeks, sliced
1 fennel bulb, roughly chopped
2 celery sticks, chopped
2 garlic cloves, peeled and halved
2 tablespoons tomato purée
450 ml (¾ pint) dry white wine
100 ml (3½ fl oz) brandy
600 ml (1 pint) fish stock
1 tablespoons chopped tarragon
1 bay leaf
pinch of cayenne pepper
1 teaspoon smoked paprika

First make the sauce. Melt the butter in a large saucepan. Add the shallots, carrots, leeks, fennel, celery and garlic. Cover and gently fry for 15 minutes, stirring occasionally. Stir in the tomato purée, wine and brandy. Bring to the boil and reduce by half. Add the stock, herbs and spices and simmer for 20 minutes. Sieve the liquid into a clean pan, discarding the vegetables.

To make the dish, reheat the sauce, adding the fish and cooked vegetables. Simmer until the fish flakes and the shellfish open. Stir in the tomatoes, parsley and lemon juice, and season with salt and pepper. Stir in the cream just before serving. Serve with garlic ciabatta and garlic mayonnaise, if liked.

seared steak

with parmesan and rocket

PREP: 10 MINUTES
COOKING TIME: 7–8 MINUTES
SERVES: 4

3 tablespoons olive oil

2 red onions, thickly sliced

500 g (1 lb) sirloin steak, cut into
   8 steaks

150 g (5 oz) rocket

125 g (4 oz) Parmesan cheese
   shavings

3 tablespoons flat leaf parsley

2 tablespoons balsamic vinegar

pepper

When the mood for red meat hits you, only a steak will do. With lashings of red onions and the classic rocket and Parmesan combination, you won't even miss the chips – honestly.

Heat 1 tablespoon oil in a frying pan over a medium heat. Add the onions and cook for 5 minutes or until golden. Remove the onions from the pan and set aside.

Increase the heat to high and add the steaks to the frying pan. Cook briefly, no more than 1 minute on each side, until sealed and seared.

Toss together the rocket, Parmesan, parsley, balsamic vinegar, black pepper and the remaining olive oil.

Put a steak on each serving plate, add some of the salad mixture, then a second steak and top with fried onions.

mustard
lamb fillet

PREP: 5 MINUTES
COOKING TIME: ABOUT
10–15 MINUTES
SERVES: 4

4 garlic cloves, crushed

2 tablespoon Dijon or English
    mustard

2 tablespoons chopped mint

1 tablespoon chopped fresh
    coriander

1 tablespoon olive oil

500 g (1 lb) neck fillet of lamb

steamed vegetables, to serve

Tender pink lamb with garlic is a match made in heaven. Add to this a fiery blast of mustard and some fresh herbs and – hey presto! – you have a dinner-party dish to impress.

Mix together the garlic, mustard, mint, coriander and oil until well combined.

Trim the lamb of any fat, rub the meat with the garlic and mustard mixture and place it in a baking dish.

Bake the lamb in a preheated oven, 200°C (400°F), Gas Mark 6, for 10–15 minutes or until it is cooked to your liking. Allow the meat to stand for 10 minutes and serve with a selection of steamed vegetables.

Sir Terence Conran's

eton mess

‘ There seems to be some argument as to whether this was a pudding invented by the eponymous college. It doesn't really matter how it came into being – it is one of the finest and, indeed, simplest of puddings. ’

PREP: 30 MINUTES
COOKING TIME: 2–2½ HOURS
SERVES: 6–8

500 g (1 lb) strawberries, sliced
50 g (2 oz) sugar
500 ml (17 fl oz) double cream,
    chilled

Meringue
6 egg whites
a pinch of salt
a pinch of cream of tartar
350 g (11½ oz) caster sugar

This recipe for meringue will make more than you will need for Eton mess, but meringue keeps very well, wrapped in tissue paper, in an airtight cake tin.

Make the meringue. Line a large baking sheet with nonstick baking parchment. Beat the egg whites, salt and cream of tartar in a large bowl until the whites are stiff but not too dry. While you are beating, allow 250 g (8 oz) sugar to drift on to the whites and continue beating until the mixture is stiff and glossy. Fold in the remaining sugar.

Place large spoonfuls of the meringue on the baking sheet, making them round, oval or whatever shape you fancy. You can make a large pavlova if you want. Put the baking sheet in a preheated oven, 110°C (225°F), Gas Mark ¼, for 2 hours. Take a look and see if the meringues are sufficiently dry – if not, leave them for another 30 minutes. Remove the meringues from the oven and transfer to a wire rack to cool.

Place the strawberries in a glass or ceramic bowl and dredge with the vanilla sugar.

Pour the cream into the bowl in which you will serve the pudding and beat it until it is lightly whipped. Fold the strawberries and meringues into the cream – it should be faintly marbled. Serve immediately.

mini kiwifruit
pavlovas

PREP: 20 MINUTES
COOKING TIME: 25–26 MINUTES
MAKES: 20 PAVLOVAS

2 egg whites
125 g (4 oz) caster sugar
drop of vanilla extract
icing sugar, to dust

Topping
50 ml (2 fl oz) double cream
1 tablespoon caster sugar
1 kiwifruit, peeled and sliced

Kiwi seeds were brought to New Zealand from China in the early 1900s. However, it's the flightless bird and not the fruit that's the national symbol of the country.

Line a baking sheet with nonstick baking paper. Put the egg whites in a clean bowl and whisk with an electric or rotary whisk until softly peaked. Add the sugar, 1 tablespoon at a time, whisking well after each addition. Continue to whisk until the mixture is thick and glossy, then fold in the vanilla extract.

Using the tips of 2 teaspoons, put 20 walnut-sized spoonfuls on the baking sheet, spacing them well apart. With the back of a teaspoon make an indentation in the centre of each one. Place in a preheated oven, 180ºC (350ºF), Gas Mark 4, for 5–6 minutes, then reduce the heat to 120ºC (250ºF), Gas Mark ½, and bake for 20 minutes until firm. Allow to cool completely, then lift the meringues from the paper.

Whip the cream and sugar until softly peaked. Put the meringues on a serving platter and place a small teaspoon of cream in the centre of each one, then top with a couple of slices of kiwifruit. To serve, dust the pavlovas lightly with icing sugar.

pear and
almond tart ✺

PREP: 20 MINUTES
COOKING TIME: 45–55 MINUTES
SERVES: 8

500 g (1 lb) shortcrust pastry,
    thawed if frozen
125 g (4 oz) butter
125 g (4 oz) sugar
1 egg, beaten
25 g (1 oz) ground almonds
25 g (1 oz) ground rice
½ teaspoon almond extract
2 x 411 g (13½ oz) can pear
    halves, drained
icing sugar, to dust

Roll out the pastry on a lightly floured surface and use it to line a lightly greased 23 cm (9 inch) fluted flan tin or dish.

Melt the butter in a saucepan and stir in the sugar. Remove from the heat and add the egg, ground almonds, ground rice and almond extract. Stir until the mixture has a dropping consistency (add a little milk if necessary).

Meanwhile, arrange the pear halves around the edge of the pastry case, placing them flat side down and spacing them evenly with a little gap between each half. Pour the egg mixture evenly over and around the pear halves.

Cook the tart in a preheated oven, 160°C (325°F), Gas Mark 3, for 45 minutes. It should be firm to the touch, but if it is not cook for a further 5–10 minutes. Leave to cool a little before easing the tart from the tin.

Dust with icing sugar and serve warm or cold.

mini chocolate and
cardamom pots

PREP: 12 MINUTES, PLUS CHILLING
COOKING TIME: 8 MINUTES
SERVES: 4

8–10 cardamom pods
200 g (7 oz) plain chocolate
   (minimum 70% cocoa solids),
   broken into squares
2 tablespoons coffee liqueur
2 tablespoons extra virgin
   olive oil
3 large eggs, separated

To serve
whipped cream
coffee-flavoured chocolates

Remove the cardamom seeds from their pods and crush to a powder using a pestle and mortar.

Put the chocolate squares in a small, heatproof bowl with the ground cardamom, coffee liqueur and olive oil and set over a pan of barely simmering water. Leave the chocolate to melt very slowly without stirring for about 8 minutes.

Remove the bowl of chocolate from the heat and quickly beat in the egg yolks. Set aside while you put the egg whites in a large bowl and whisk until stiff. Stir 1 tablespoon of the beaten eggs into the chocolate mixture to slacken it, then carefully fold in the remaining egg whites with a metal spoon.

Spoon the mixture into 4 ramekins. Cover and chill in the refrigerator for about 2 hours until set, then serve with a little whipped cream and some crushed coffee-flavoured chocolates.

sticky toffee
pudding ❀

PREP: 20 MINUTES
COOKING TIME: 30 MINUTES
SERVES: 8–10

Sponge
125 g (4 oz) soft margarine, plus
    extra for greasing
175 g (6 oz) ready-to-eat dates,
    chopped
1 teaspoon bicarbonate of soda
300 ml (½ pint) boiling water
175 g (6 oz) soft brown sugar
250 g (8 oz) wholemeal or white
    self-raising flour
1 teaspoon baking powder
2 eggs, lightly beaten

Sauce
150 g (5 oz) caster sugar
75 g (3 oz) unsalted butter
150 ml (¼ pint) double cream

Lightly grease a 20 x 30 x 3.5 cm (8 x 12 x 1½ inch) baking tin. Put the dates in a bowl with the bicarbonate of soda, cover with 300 ml (½ pint) boiling water and leave to cool.

Cream together the margarine and sugar until they are pale in colour. Add the flour and baking powder and then beat in the eggs, a few spoonfuls at a time.

When the date mixture has cooled but is still warm, add it to the cake mixture and combine well. (The mixture will be like a thin batter.) Pour the mixture into the prepared tin and bake in preheated oven, 160°C (325°F), Gas Mark 3, for 30–35 minutes or until the sponge is firm to the touch and pulling away from around the edges of the tin.

Meanwhile, make the sauce. Put the sugar, butter and cream in a heavy-based saucepan and heat, stirring, over a gentle heat until the mixture is smooth and the sugar has dissolved. Leave the sauce to cool a little, then pour the warm sauce over the still-warm cooked sponge.

❛ After my diagnosis many friends and family came to visit me. This was a simple dish that I found really easy to prepare for them. ❜
Irene Mackay, diagnosed 2006

cherry tomato
tartlets

PREP: 10 MINUTES
COOKING TIME: 18 MINUTES
SERVES: 4

375 g (12 oz) cherry tomatoes
2 tablespoons olive oil
1 onion, finely chopped
2 garlic cloves, crushed
3 tablespoons sun-dried tomato
   purée
325 g (11 oz) puff pastry, thawed
   if frozen
beaten egg, to glaze

Crème fraîche pesto
150 g (5 oz) crème fraîche
2 tablespoons pesto
salt and pepper

Lightly oil a baking sheet and sprinkle with water. Halve 150 g (5 oz) of the tomatoes.

Heat the oil in a frying pan, add the onion and fry for about 3 minutes or until soft. Take the pan off the heat, add the garlic and tomato purée, then stir in all the tomatoes.

Roll out the pastry on a lightly floured surface and cut out 4 circles, each 12 cm (5 inches) across, using a small bowl as a guide. Place on the baking sheet and make a shallow cut 1 cm (½ inch) from the edge of each circle to make a rim. Brush the rims with beaten egg. Pile the tomato mixture in the centres of the pastries, making sure the mixture stays within the rims.

Bake the tartlets in a preheated oven, 220°C (425°F), Gas Mark 7, for about 15 minutes until the pastry has risen and is golden.

Meanwhile, mix together the crème fraîche, pesto and salt and pepper in a bowl so that the crème fraîche is streaked with the pesto. Transfer the tartlets to a plate and add a generous dollop of the crème fraîche pesto to each one.

charred artichoke, olive and parma ham
tartlets

PREP: 25 MINUTES
COOKING TIME: 22–27 MINUTES
SERVES: 4

4 small marinated artichoke
  hearts, halved
1 tablespoon olive oil
12 thin slices of Parma ham
4 large eggs
125 g (4 oz) ricotta cheese
50 g (2 oz) pitted black olives,
  roughly chopped
2–3 spring onions, thinly sliced
½ tablespoon chopped chives
1 tablespoon chopped basil
½ tablespoon chopped tarragon
salt and pepper

To garnish
shredded basil leaves
toasted hazelnuts

Heat a griddle pan over a moderately high heat and brush the halved artichoke hearts all over with the olive oil. When the pan is hot put the artichoke hearts, cut side down, in the pan and leave to char for about 2 minutes. Turn off the heat, use tongs to remove the artichokes and put them, cut side up, on a plate. Set aside.

Cut 4 of the Parma ham slices into thin shreds and cut the remaining slices in half. Use the halved slices to line 8 sections of a muffin tin.

Lightly beat the eggs in a large bowl, then beat in the ricotta until smooth. Stir in the olives, spring onions, chives, basil, tarragon and shredded ham and season well with pepper and a pinch of salt.

Spoon the egg mixture into the 8 muffin moulds; they should all be about two-thirds full. Place an artichoke half, cut side up, in the centre of each tartlet, so that the charred side is showing.

Bake the tartlets in a preheated oven, 200°C (400°F), Gas Mark 6, for 20–25 minutes until they are golden and firm to the touch. Remove the tartlets from the oven and leave to cool in the tin for a few minutes. Carefully remove them from the tin and serve garnished with shredded basil leaves and sprinkled with a few chopped, toasted hazelnuts.

Rachel Allen's
sponge cake with rhubarb cream

" This is a classic Victoria sponge, made all the more gorgeous by the rhubarb cream filling. Also try filling it with raspberry jam and whipped cream, sliced strawberries and whipped cream, or with fresh, hand-picked blackberries and cream. This is perfect for Father's or Mother's Day or, of course, as a birthday cake! "

PREP: 20 MINUTES
COOKING TIME: 20–25 MINUTES
SERVES: 6–8

125 g (4 oz) butter, softened
175 g (6 oz) caster sugar
3 eggs
175 g (6 oz) plain flour
1 teaspoon baking powder
1 tablespoon milk
icing sugar or caster sugar, for
    dusting

Rhubarb cream
100 g (3½ oz) rhubarb, trimmed
    and sliced
50 g (2 oz) caster sugar
4 tablespoons water
75 ml (3 fl oz) double cream

Grease and base-line two 18 cm (7 inch) cake tins and grease and flour the sides.

Put the butter in a bowl and cream until soft. Gradually add the sugar and beat until light and fluffy. Add the eggs one at a time, beating well between each addition.

Sieve together the flour and baking powder and stir gently into the egg mixture. Stir in the milk until just combined.

Spoon the mixture into the prepared tins, hollowing it slightly in the centre. Bake in a preheated oven, 180°C (350°F), Gas Mark 4, for 20–25 minutes or until the centre of the cakes spring back when you press them gently with your fingertips. Turn out on to a wire rack and leave to cool. (Make sure that the cake that will be the top layer is on its base so that the top isn't marked by the rack.)

Meanwhile, put the rhubarb, sugar and 4 tablespoons water in a small saucepan, cover and cook gently for about 10 minutes or until the rhubarb is soft. Take off the lid and boil, stirring, until it is thick. Pour into a bowl and leave to cool. Whip the cream until if forms soft peaks, then fold in the rhubarb.

Sandwich the cakes with the rhubarb cream and sprinkle with sieved icing or caster sugar.

classic pimm's

PREP: 3 MINUTES
NO COOK
SERVES: 1

The drink of the summer ... all you need is the sunshine to go with it!

1 measure Pimm's No. 1

3–4 ice cubes

2–3 slices of orange, lemon and cucumber

3 measures lemonade

Pour the Pimm's into a tall glass and add the ice cubes.

Add the fruit and cucumber slices, then add the lemonade.

kiwifruit, grape and
lime crush

PREP: 5 MINUTES
NO COOK
SERVES: 3–4

250 g (8 oz) kiwifruit, peeled

300 ml (½ pint) white grape juice

juice of 2 limes

crushed ice, to serve

kiwifruit slices, to decorate

Put the kiwifruit, grape juice and lime juice in a food processor and process until smooth.

Serve in glasses over crushed ice and decorate with slices of kiwifruit.

jersey lily

PREP: 5 MINUTES
NO COOK
SERVES: 1

150 ml (¼ pint) sparkling apple
    juice
2 dashes Angostura bitters
¼ teaspoon caster sugar
ice cubes
cocktail cherry, to decorate

Sparkling grape juice, either red or white, will make a refreshing substitute for the apple juice.

Put the apple juice, bitters, sugar and ice cubes in a cocktail shaker.

Shake well, then strain into a wine glass. Decorate with a cocktail cherry.

nursery fizz

PREP: 5 MINUTES
NO COOK
SERVES: 1

crushed ice
orange juice
ginger ale

To decorate
cocktail cherry
orange slice

Fill a large wine glass with crushed ice and pour in equal measures of orange juice and ginger ale.

Decorate with a cocktail cherry and an orange slice speared on to a cocktail stick. Serve with a straw.

index

acknowledgements

Every reasonable effort has been made to acknowledge the ownership of copyright material included in this book. Any errors that have inadvertently occurred will be corrected in subsequent editions providing notification has been sent to the publisher.

The publishers and Breast Cancer Care would like to thank the following for contributing recipes to this book:
Rachel Allen 246-247 (Sponge Cake with Rhubarb Cream from *Rachel's Favourite Food at Home*. Published in 2006 by Harper Collins of London) ; Anjum Anand 174-175; Snober Bhangu 113; Julia Bradbury 167; Helen Brahmbhatt 63; Fern Britton 209, 220-221; Rosemary Conley 144-145; Sir Terence Conran 238-239; Kristin Cooke 217; Pauline Davidson 215; Marion Daw 241; Sara Donaldson 121; Lotte Duncan 117, 231; Catriona Edwards 95; Sharon Eglash 41; Rose Elliot 44-45, 78-79; Lisa Faulkner 212-213; Ursula Ferrigno 106-107, 200-201; Romalo Garai 219; Rose Gray 58-59 (Sea Bass Baked in Salt from *River Café Pocket Book: Fish*, published by Ebury Press, 2006); Ainsley Harriott 90-91 (Crispy Corned Beef and Beet Hash from *Ainsley Harriott's Feel-Good Cookbook* by Ainsley Harriott, published by BBC Books. Reprinted by permission of The Random House Group Ltd.); Nigel Havers 138-139; Alan Hobson 191; Hugh Johnson 74-75; Gemma Jones 101; Jenny Jones 135; Lorraine Kelly 87; Margaret Knight 225; Tessa Kottler 203; Eric Lanlard 199; Rula Lenska 123; Irene Mackay 173, 243; Nan McDonald 211; Jacky Merrison 147; Laura Miller 25; Sir Patrick Moore 100; Diana Moran 12; Jamie Oliver 182-183 (© Jamie Oliver 2007. All rights reserved); Marguerite Patten 148-149; Marion Pattison 163; Suzanne Price 37; Samia al Qadhi 143; Esther Rantzen 131; Simon Rimmer 234-235; Mike Robinson 196-197; Shila Sampat 109; Gail Simon 83; Kim Smith 169; Sue Smith 103; Paula Snow 69; Rick Stein 35; Gill Swain-Coad 127; Antony Worrall Thompson 206-207; Linda Thurlow 125; Dr Ann-Marie Todd 160; Mitchell Tonks 171; Phil Vickery 150-151; Greg Wallace 158-159; Denise Welch 52-53, 89; Susan Woodcock 73, 222; Sarah Young 227.

Executive editor Jane Donovan
Editor Emma Pattison
Executive art editor Penny Stock
Designer Peter Gerrish
Illustrator Natacha Ledwidge
Senior production controller
Martin Croshaw

- **Rachel Allen** – TV chef, presenter (*Rachel's Favourite Food*, *Rachel's Favourite Food For Friends* and *Rachel's Favourite Food At Home*) and food writer.
- **Anjum Anand** – Author of *Indian Everyday – Light Healthy Indian Food* (Headline). Television appearances include *Great Food Live* and *Taste*.
- **Julia Bradbury** – TV presenter (*Watchdog*, *Top Gear*, GMTV, *National Lottery*, *Wish You Were Here*, *Just the Two of Us*, *Wainwright's Walks*).
- **Fern Britton** – *This Morning*
- **Rosemary Conley CBE** – Diet and fitness expert, TV Presenter and author of 30 books and videos/DVD's and founder of Rosemary Conley Diet & Fitness Clubs and Magazine.
- **Sir Terence Conran** – Founder of Habitat and The Conran Shop,

renowned restaurateur and food writer.

• **Lotte Duncan** – TV chef/presenter and English country cook (*Castle in the Country*, *Great Food Live*).

• **Rose Elliot** – Food writer. Has led the way in revolutionizing vegetarian cooking and played a key role in transforming the image, taste and popularity of vegetarian food.

• **Lisa Faulkner** – Actress (*Holby City* and *Spooks*).

• **Ursula Ferrigno** – Food writer specializing in Italian food with numerous books and TV appearances to her name; also runs courses at Books for Cooks.

• **Romola Garai** – Actress (*I Capture the Castle*, *Nicholas Nickleby*, *Daniel Deronda*, *Angel*, *As You Like It*).

• **Rose Gray** – Co-founder of the River Café. Restaurateur, food writer (The River Café Cookbooks) and Ambassador for Breast Cancer Care.

• **Ainsley Harriott** – TV chef, presenter (*Ready Steady Cook*) and food writer.

• **Nigel Havers** – Actor (*Chariots of Fire*, *A Passage to India*, *Empire of the Sun*, *A Horseman Riding By*, *The Charmer*, *Little Britain*).

• **Hugh Johnson** – one of the world's bestselling authors on wine and gardening. His books include *The World Atlas of Wine*, *The Story of Wine* and *The International Book of Trees*.

• **Gemma Jones** – Actress (*Bridget Jones' Diary/Bridget Jones: The Edge of Reason*, *Sense and Sensibility*, *Harry Potter*).

• **Lorraine Kelly** – GMTV presenter, *Sun* columnist and *Best* magazine agony aunt.

• **Eric Lanlard** – Protégé of Albert Roux and patissier to the stars including Madonna and Victoria and David Beckham. Author of *Glamour Cakes* (Hamlyn, 2008). Owner of Savoir Design and Cake Boy in Battersea.

• **Rula Lenska** – Actress and conservationist.

• **Sir Patrick Moore** – Astronomer and presenter of BBC's *The Sky at Night*.

• **Diana Moran** – The Green Goddess, TV presenter, broadcaster and author.

• **Jamie Oliver** – Chef, presenter, campaigner and author of seven internationally bestselling books (*The Naked Chef*, *The Return of the Naked Chef*, *Happy Days with the Naked Chef*, *Jamie's Kitchen*, *Jamie's Dinners*, *Jamie's Italy* and *Cook With Jamie*).

• **Marguerite Patten OBE** – Food writer and home economist with almost 170 books to her name. Doyenne of food writers and original TV celebrity cook.

• **Esther Rantzen** – TV broadcaster and presenter

• **Simon Rimmer** – TV chef/presenter (*Something for the Weekend* and *Grubs Up*), owner of Greens, the celebrated vegetarian restaurant in Manchester, and Earle, in Hale, and author of *The Accidental Vegetarian* and *Rebel Cook*.

• **Mike Robinson** – TV chef/presenter (*Heaven's Kitchen* and *Safari Chef*), Owner of The Pot Kiln near Newbury.

• **Rick Stein** – TV chef/presenter. Owner of the world-renowned restaurant The Seafood Restaurant with 10 cookery books to his name.

• **Mitch Tonks** – Founder of Fishworks restaurants. Television appearances include *Horizon*, *Great Food Live* and *Saturday Kitchen*.

• **Phil Vickery** – TV presenter and food writer (*Ready Steady Cook*, *This Morning*).

• **Gregg Wallace** – TV chef (*Saturday Kitchen*, *MasterChef*) with regular columns in *Olive* and BBC *Good Food* magazines.

• **Denise Welch** – Actress (*Waterloo Road*, *Coronation Street*, *Holby City*, *Hollyoaks*, *The Bill*).

• **Antony Worrall Thompson** – restaurateur, author and TV cook (*Daily Cooks*, *Saturday Cooks*), Journalist – Express Newspapers.

about Breast Cancer Care

Every day more than 100 people are told that they have breast cancer. Breast Cancer Care is there to offer dedicated support to these people and their families, 24 hours a day, seven days a week, via a range of free services. Through its confidential helpline, online chat forums, one-to-one support sessions and face-to-face activities it offers the chance to talk to someone who has 'been there' and who has experienced breast cancer themselves. In addition, its highly specialized team provides all the latest knowledge and information through the website, booklets and fact sheets to help people understand their diagnosis and the choices they have.

Every year Breast Cancer Care responds to more than two million requests for support and information about breast cancer or breast health concerns.

If you, or someone you know, is going through breast cancer or has a breast health concern please do call the Breast Cancer Care helpline free on 0808 800 6000 (for Typetalk prefix 18001), or for more information visit www.breastcancercare.org.uk, where you can also find the contact details for your nearest Breast Cancer Care centre and other ways you can support the charity.

BREAST CANCER CARE